IMAGES
*of America*

# HACKLEBARNEY AND
# VOORHEES STATE PARKS

Alden Whitman once wrote, "Our ideals, laws and customs should be based on the proposition that each generation in turn becomes the custodian rather than the absolute owner of our resources and each generation has the obligation to pass this inheritance on to the future." So it is with Hacklebarney and Voorhees State Parks—it is our duty to pass those resources on to our children, our grandchildren, and their children, just as the young men of the Civilian Conservation Corps did from 1933 to 1941. (Courtesy Albert Peterson Jr.)

IMAGES
*of America*

# HACKLEBARNEY AND
# VOORHEES STATE PARKS

Peter Osborne

ARCADIA

First published 2004


Published by Arcadia Publishing,
Charleston SC, Chicago IL, Portsmouth NH, San Francisco CA

Printed in Great Britain

Library of Congress Catalog Card Number: 2004108754

For all general information, contact Arcadia Publishing:
Telephone 843-853-2070
Fax 843-853-0044
E-mail sales@arcadiapublishing.com
For customer service and orders:
Toll-free 1-888-313-2665

Visit us on the Internet at www.arcadiapublishing.com

*To my wife and editor, Janis,*
*and to Beth, Gary, Lauren, Rachel, GP, Kerrie, Meaghan, Christina,*
*Mary, Steve, Steve Jr., Andrew,*
*and my mother.*

The following publishers have generously given permission to use illustrations from their copyrighted works: *We Can Take It: A Short History of the* CCC, by Ray Hoyt, copyright 1999, and reprinted by permission of Basil Nickerson. *Your CCC: A Handbook For Enrollees,* copyright 1999, and reprinted by permission of Basil Nickerson. Camp Newsletters, Company No. 1268, and reprinted by permission of the Center for Research Libraries, Chicago, Illinois. National Archives and Records Administration, Records Group 35.

The pick and shovel were among the tools the CCC used to create Hacklebarney and Voorhees State Parks. (Reprinted from *We Can Take It: A Short Story of the CCC.*)

# CONTENTS

# ACKNOWLEDGMENTS

Without the following people, institutions, and agencies, I could not have completed this work. First, I wish to acknowledge my wife, Janis, who edited copy and was supportive, as always.

I am greatly in the debt of Patricia A. Cianflone, the superintendent at Voorhees and Hacklebarney State Parks. She deserves five gold stars for her enthusiasm and great desire to remember the Civilian Conservation Corps (CCC) boys and to preserve the parks' histories. Always gracious and helpful, she allowed me access to the parks' archives, from which the majority of the photographs in this book come, read various versions of the manuscript, and spent hours on research. She and members of her able staff—Nancy Diekroger, chief ranger; Robert Bork, ranger; Kathleen Daku, customer service representative; George Krapf, Wilhelm Roethel Jr., and Jack Compton, the maintenance crew at Voorhees; and Walter Rittger, the maintenance man at Hacklebarney—collectively, provided one of the best examples there is in the state on how to preserve the memory of the CCC.

Members of the New Jersey Division of Parks and Forestry also provided a great deal of help, specifically Charles Sary, superintendent of Monmouth Battlefield State Park; Inga Gabliks, superintendent of Allaire State Park; Stephen Ellis, regional superintendent; Kevin Wright, regional resource interpretive specialist, northern region; Elizabeth Dowd, regional resource interpretive specialist, central region; Beverly Weaver, resource interpretive specialist in the Trenton office; Bob Opacki, principal drafting technician; Pete Straw and David Eckwielen, former superintendents; and Michael Monahan, Voorhees Residential Group Center.

Friends of the park who assisted include Judy Beckwith; Amanda and Mark DiRienz; Doug Kiovsky, assistant park planner for the Hunterdon County Department of Parks and Recreation; Ali McGaheran; Steve Kallesser of Gracie & Harrigan Consulting Foresters; Albert Mastriani; the New Jersey Astronomical Association; John W. Mount, the president of the New Jersey Astronomical Association; Sparky Nanni; Jack Woollis; Wanda Jacobson; Barbara Morse; Patricia Morse; Joan Fairchild; North Jersey Highlands Historical Society; Kay Environmental Center; Nature Conservancy Field Service; Savage Arms Inc.; John Parichuk; Chester Barwick; James Ashey Jr.; Joseph Richardson; Albert Peterson Jr.; Anthony Capizzi; Mickey Nalence; Ernest Nixon; Michael Nalavany; Bruce De Bacco; Lance Metz; the National Canal Museum; Dorothy Razawich; Alma Thompson; Ralph Voorhees; and Gina Gray Bryan, who provided several much sought-after photographs of the Borie family. Joan Case and the Chester Historical Society provided a great deal of assistance with research requests.

Members of the board of directors at the Minisink Valley Historical Society were supportive, as always. The society's finest volunteer historical researcher, Nancy Conod, gets five gold stars for helping with many research requests, reading the manuscript, and offering much needed advice. A good deal of the genealogical and historical data on the Borie and Voorhees families is a result of her research. Nancy Vocci traveled to conduct research and also gets gold stars. Florence Gray, Margie Sierski, and Mirial Haubner also assisted with research and found valuable pieces of information. Charles King provided help in identifying machinery used by the CCC. Brian Lewis, my administrative assistant, helped with identifying and laying out the CCC camp. Cyndi and Dave Wood provided a rare photograph. Mary and Mead Stapler, friends for many years, offered encouragement and valuable assistance.

Basil Nickerson kindly gave permission to use previously copyrighted materials. The illustrations from the camp newsletters are reproduced from CCC Camp Papers, held by the Center for Research Libraries, and for permission to use them, we are grateful. The staff and members of the National Association of Civilian Conservation Corps Alumni provided assistance. The National Archives and Records Administration allowed the use of graphic materials.

# Introduction

This is a book about two important developments in New Jersey's history: first, the creation and history of two of its popular state parks, Voorhees and Hacklebarney, and second, the largest national conservation movement ever undertaken in the United States. The creation of Voorhees and Hacklebarney State Parks was part of a national movement from 1910 to 1940 that has been called the golden age of parks. It was a time when many local, county, state, and national parks and forests were established and developed all across the country. The creation of both Voorhees and Hacklebarney State Parks was the result of a combination of acts of generosity, grand design work, beautiful vistas, scenic places, and the fruition of a president's and a youth work program's vision—a vision whose legacy still lives on, some 70 years later.

The 1920s witnessed several other major developments that came together as Americans yearned for open spaces, due to the increased urbanization taking place across the land. Automobiles were becoming available to the average American, and as a result, Americans began a great love affair with the road. The Boy Scout and Girl Scout movements, established in 1910 and 1912, respectively, blossomed and needed places to conduct outdoor programs. During this era both organizations grew rapidly and flourished.

In this same time period, a huge, unprecedented conservation effort was begun by the United States, the likes of which has never been undertaken since. As part of that effort, some 1,000 young men worked at Voorhees and Hacklebarney from 1933 to 1941, in a federal agency known as the Civilian Conservation Corps. The Depression-era CCC was the brainchild of one of the 20th century's leading figures, Pres. Franklin Delano Roosevelt. The agency had two goals: to give jobs to unemployed young men between the ages of 17 and 24, as well as to veterans of World War I, and to undertake thousands of conservation projects across the nation in parks, in forests, and at historic sites.

When the CCC boys arrived at Voorhees in 1933, they found three relatively undeveloped parcels of land. They worked under the supervision of the National Park Service and the U.S. Army, and by the time they were finished eight years later, they had built the present-day road systems, shelters, latrines, visitor amenities, and trail systems and had developed major public access areas that still remain, although some are used in different ways today. The CCC's work remains the single greatest conservation effort ever undertaken at either Voorhees or Hacklebarney. Some of the projects have fallen into disrepair or are gone, like the extensive water system installed at Hacklebarney and two of the picnic pavilions that were once located in Voorhees, but the parks we enjoy today are largely the result of their efforts.

Since the end of the CCC, the parks have continued on with their mission, and the state has regularly upgraded facilities at both locations. Today, more than 100,000 visitors come to each of the parks annually. Because of generous neighboring landowners and the Green Acres program, the parks have grown in size. Voorhees has more than doubled its original size and is now 640 acres. Two other satellite properties totalling 402 acres have recently been acquired. Hacklebarney began as a 32-acre parcel and now encompasses 977 acres.

The two parks are still jewels in the crown of the park system, particularly for the region's residents. Voorhees and Hacklebarney, however, like all of the state's parks and forests, have had budgets cut in a way that continues to hurt them and us—the parks' owners and users. A good example of this occurred in 1981, some 46 years after the donation of lands that created Hacklebarney, when there was serious consideration given to closing the park because of a budget crisis. One of the purposes of this book is to encourage elected officials and government leaders to fund parks and forests in a more adequate fashion and to impress upon those leaders the parks' importance to the people of New Jersey.

It is also worth remembering the many people who have made the parks possible, including the landowners who gave land directly to the state, sold it, deeded it through the Green Acres program or, in several cases, had property taken by condemnation. For Voorhees State Park they include Foster M. Voorhees, Dora Deutsch, Ellis Anderson, Arthur Lance, Lewis Lance, Addie Lance, and Nancy Lance, Bessie Anderson, Wallace Morris, Joan and Edwin Wack, Fritz Blum and Hans Peyer, Celeste Barnes, Gladys Smith, Jean and Frank Valinski, Evelyn and Harold Brynildsen, the Estate of L. Kielb and F. Biggs, Janet and Larry Berkey, Jan Willoughby, Mary Sekela and various Sekela family members, R. Scott and Karen Conant, Ava Herzog and Elsie Sutton, Richard Pfauth, Marbow Manor, Kathy and Harry Creveling, George Dorsey, Hannah Fitzpatrick, Joann and Albert Cutter, September Farms, and the Herson Family Trust. For Hacklebarney they are Adolphe and Sarah Borie, Annette and James Hildebrant, Lloyd Hildebrant, Jane and Chester Burley, Marion and Nicholas Dawson, Sterling Security Corporation-Bassett Foundation, Marion and Frank Kopp, Anita Merle-Knight Smith, Vernon Hoffman, Elizabeth and Richard Morash, Olivia and Wayne Nordberg, W. J. B. Contractors, Brady Security & Realty, Black River Fish & Game Club, and James and Augustus Knight.

We tip our hats to Pres. Franklin Roosevelt, to the federal agencies that coordinated the CCC effort, and to the hard work and dedication of the CCC boys. We remember the members of the Youth Conservation Corps and Young Adult Conservation Corps and the many men and women of the Division of Parks and Forestry who have worked at both parks over the years. They are too numerous to mention by name, but their hard work has maintained and preserved the parks for the people. Finally, we acknowledge the people of New Jersey, who provide the funding for the operations of the state's parks and forests.

As you read this book, you will also see that the need for a program similar to the CCC still exists, not only for the benefit of our youth but also for our parks and forests, which need the loving care, maintenance, and nurturing the CCC gave them 70 years ago. These places are, after all, the people's parks and forests.

—Peter Osborne
Executive Director, Minisink Valley Historical Society
Port Jervis, New York

# One

# HACKLEBARNEY MEMORIAL STATE FOREST PARK RESERVATION

Deep in the ravines of Trout and Rinehart Brooks are remote places that belie the fact that, within a short distance, sweeping suburban sprawl is closing in on Hacklebarney State Park. One can view the glacial moraine of millennia ago, when an ice sheet covered the region. The rock strewn landscape is all that remains of that major geological event; it is also a place that is endowed with a fascinating history.

It is said the word Hacklebarney has a Native American derivation. Depending on which source one reads, it may have come from the words *haki*, meaning "ground" and *barney*, a variation of *bohihen*, "to put wood on fire," or *hackiboni*, "to put wood on a fire on the ground" or "bonfire." Other explanations come by way of the area's iron-mining history. The first concerns an iron mine foreman named Barney Tracey, who was lovingly but persistently heckled by his workmen—hence the name "Heckle" Barney. Another tradition says the name came from the Irish miners and their home village in Cork County. Finally, the land near the Hacklebarney forge may have been owned by a Barney Hackle.

Whatever the origin of its name, we do know that the Hacklebarney Memorial State Forest Park Reservation, or Hacklebarney State Park, as it is now called, was established because of the generosity and vision of Adolphe and Sarah Borie. Their vision for Hacklebarney has endured long after their deaths and continues to guide the destiny of the park once described as "the most beautiful park in New Jersey."

The region in which both parks are located was once inhabited by Native Americans. Over thousands of years, they developed from a hunting culture to a hunting and gathering society, and then to an agricultural one known as the Lenni Lenape. Evidence of the Lenni Lenape in the form of mushpots—worn, scooped-out surfaces in the rock, used for grinding foodstuffs—can still be seen along the Black River. (Courtesy Minisink Valley Historical Society.)

The highlights of the rocky and rugged landscape of Hacklebarney are the falls at Trout and Rinehart Brooks and the cascading Black River. The Black River, also known as the Lamington or Alamatuck, runs the full length of Morris County and cuts through the center of Hacklebarney State Park. Its name is said to derive from Native Americans, and means "black rock bottom" or "black earth bottom." (Courtesy Chester Historical Society.)

By the time European settlers were moving into the region in the 1730s, few Native Americans remained. This house, on Hacklebarney Road on the Black River, is one of the oldest in the area and probably was home to the family that operated the mill across the road. Within two miles of the house lies the survey line that divided the colonies of East and West Jersey. (Courtesy Voorhees State Park.)

Beginning in the early 18th century and continuing until recent decades, the area was largely an agriculturally based economy, with larger communities located at Chester, Clinton, and High Bridge. The rolling landscape was home to many farms that were operated by the same families for generations. (Courtesy Chester Historical Society.)

As the area developed, a number of mills were built along the Black River to service the area's farmers and residents. These included grist, saw, machine, and woolen mills. The Hacklebarney Mill was used for grinding corn and grains, and a sawmill was nearby. The Hacklebarney Mill is located just outside the park boundaries, and is known to have operated from 1828 to at least 1916. (Courtesy Voorhees State Park.)

For more than 100 years, iron was mined and forged at Hacklebarney, a short distance north of the the future park site. In the late 19th century, a number of new iron mines were opened along the Black River, in Chester, and in nearby Mine Hill and Ironia. Most were shaft mines, but some were shallow surface mines. A large blast furnace in Chester created pig iron for industrial purposes. (Courtesy Chester Historical Society.)

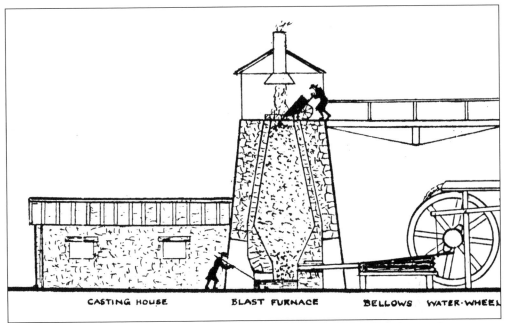

CASTING HOUSE      BLAST FURNACE      BELLOWS  WATER-WHEEL

The men who dug the ore were a rugged lot, and Chester prospered during this time, as thousands of tons of ore were processed in blast furnaces like the one shown here. (Courtesy North Jersey Highlands Historical Society.)

One of the many surface iron mines opened was called the Wortman Mine, which was named for the family on whose property it was located. The mine was not close enough to the nearby railroads, however, and it was not profitable to move the material to the furnaces, so this mine never became an important provider of ore. The remains of Wortman Mine, now on park property, can still be seen. (Courtesy Voorhees State Park.)

# CENTRAL RAILROAD OF NEW JERSEY.

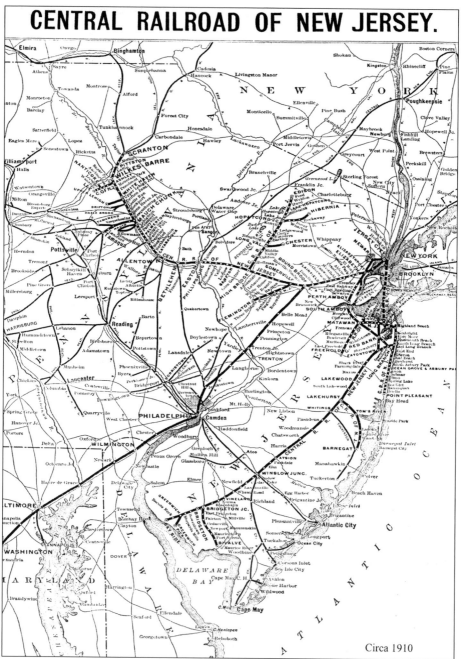

Circa 1910

Beginning in the 1820s, access into the central western region of New Jersey was dramatically improved with the construction of the Morris Canal, which shipped anthracite coal from Pennsylvania to New York. In the late 1840s, the first railroad was constructed into the Chester area, which allowed significant development of the region. When the Central Railroad of New Jersey was built, the area was soon discovered by wealthy New Yorkers and Philadelphians, who could easily commute to work by train. They began buying and creating large landed estates. One of those families was that of Adolphe E. Borie, who purchased several tracts of property bordering the Black River in Morris County. (Courtesy Minisink Valley Historical Society.)

Adolphe E. Borie was from a large family whose progenitors had emigrated from France and Haiti and settled in Philadelphia in the 1770s. The Borie family genealogy is complex. There were a large number of families, and first names were often used repeatedly in the same generations. This chart illustrates only the direct line of Adolphe Borie, the park donor. (Courtesy Nancy Conod and Nancy Vocci.)

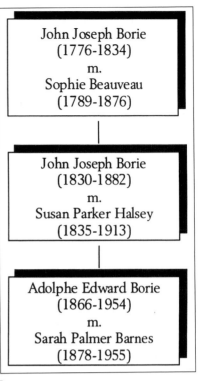

John Joseph Borie
(1776-1834)
m.
Sophie Beauveau
(1789-1876)

John Joseph Borie
(1830-1882)
m.
Susan Parker Halsey
(1835-1913)

Adolphe Edward Borie
(1866-1954)
m.
Sarah Palmer Barnes
(1878-1955)

At least two other Borie family members with the first name Adolphe achieved a degree of prominence. The first Adolphe Borie (1809–1880) was a businessman in Philadelphia and an important supporter of the Union during the Civil War. He was secretary of the navy under Pres. Ulysses S. Grant, and two World War II destroyers were named after him. Another Adolphe Borie (1877–1934), pictured here, was a well-known American artist. (Reprinted from *Adolphe Borie*.)

15

The donor of Hacklebarney State Park, Adolphe E. Borie (1866–1954), was from a family with a prominent place in American history, dating back more than two centuries. His father, John Borie, was a prominent Philadelphia lawyer and sugar manufacturer who was involved in a variety of businesses. Adolphe Borie was described in 1910 as a merchant in zinc manufacturing. He later served as president of the Savage Arms Company and vice president of Bethlehem Steel Corporation. A graduate of St. Paul's School in Concord, New Hampshire, he was a member of the Century Club in New York. He lived in several homes, including one called Bound Brook in Hempstead, New York, and another in France, where he traveled frequently. (Courtesy Gina Gray Bryan.)

Sarah Palmer Barnes (far left) married Adolphe Borie in 1919. The couple had no children but were very close to the children of John and Gina Gray, their estate caretakers. Having tea with Sarah Borie after enjoying a swim in the Black River, just behind the Borie home are, from left to right, nurse Margaret McDonald, Pearl Warren, and Phyllis Gray. (Courtesy Gina Gray Bryan.)

Sometime after 1924, Adolphe Borie moved into this large and rambling home, located in a lovely setting, with tennis courts. He is remembered by one longtime Chester resident as a soft-spoken man with an accent. Borie was given an award from the French government for his work with underprivileged children and even sponsored children who were recipients of Fresh Air Fund donations to come to Hacklebarney State Park. (Courtesy Gina Gray Bryan.)

Adolphe and Sarah Borie's farm was typical of the large landed estates of the wealthy in the late 19th and early 20th centuries. The rolling fields and pastureland, like that shown here behind the Hacklebarney Mill, became ideal locations for the wealthy to build estates. Adolphe Borie's landholdings were located in the townships of Chester and Washington, in Morris County. (Courtesy Chester Historical Society.)

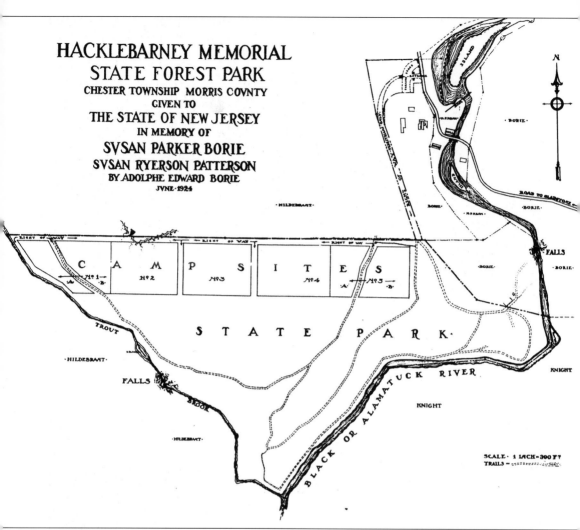

HACKLEBARNEY MEMORIAL
STATE FOREST PARK
CHESTER TOWNSHIP MORRIS COVNTY
GIVEN TO
THE STATE OF NEW JERSEY
IN MEMORY OF
SVSAN PARKER BORIE
SVSAN RYERSON PATTERSON
BY ADOLPHE EDWARD BORIE
JVNE·1924

It is not known what prompted Adolphe Borie to donate a portion of his estate to the people of New Jersey, although, at the time, there were a number of notable gifts of land dedicated for recreation purposes across the country. Nearby examples include High Point State Park and Stokes State Forest in New Jersey and Harriman State Park in New York. On June 5, 1924, Adolphe E. and Sarah P. Borie donated 32 acres of land to the people of New Jersey. The reservation was to be used for picnic grounds, a public vacation center, and a forest demonstration area. One condition of the gift was that the Borie family could camp at five specified campsites. To access the property, Borie sold a right of way across his land. From 1924 to 1937, visitors entered the park through the northeastern corner of the property. (Courtesy Voorhees State Park.)

As part of the terms of the gift, a memorial, which could take the form of a tablet, tablets, or arch, was to be erected to honor the memory of Susan Borie, the mother of Adolphe Borie, and Susan Patterson, the daughter of Adolphe Borie's sister, Emily Ryerson. Two large stone pillars, along with a large wall of cut stone, were placed at the entrance and paid for by Borie. (Courtesy Chester Historical Society.)

THIS WOODLAND IS GIVEN TO
THE STATE OF NEW JERSEY BY ADOLPHE EDWARD BORIE
TO BE FOREVER PRESERVED FOR THE BENEFIT OF YOUTH
IN MEMORY OF HIS MOTHER
1835 - SUSAN PARKER BORIE - 1913
AND HER GRANDDAUGHTER
1890 - SUSAN RYERSON PATTERSON - 1921
TWO WOMEN OF RARE VISION CHARACTER AND COURAGE
JUNE - 1924

The large bronze plaque, erected in 1924, now graces the entrance of the park, along with two small plaques inscribed with the park's name. These were taken from the former entrance and moved to this new location when the park's main entrance was moved in 1937. (Courtesy Voorhees State Park.)

Each of the women to whom Adolphe Borie dedicated the park was a special person. The first was Susan Parker Halsey Borie, his mother, with whom he must have had a special relationship. Unfortunately, little is known about her and no photographs of her have been found. A portrait of her was painted by Ellen Rand, the celebrity portrait painter of the early 20th century, which was a treasured family possession. The second woman was Susan Parker Ryerson Patterson, who was involved in two of the most dramatic events of the 20th century: the sinking of the *Titanic* and World War I. Susan Parker Ryerson was returning from France on the *Titanic* in 1912, when the ship struck an iceberg and sank. Her mother, Emily Ryerson, and two siblings, John and Emily, survived the disaster, but her father, Arthur Ryerson, perished in the Atlantic. (Courtesy Minisink Valley Historical Society.)

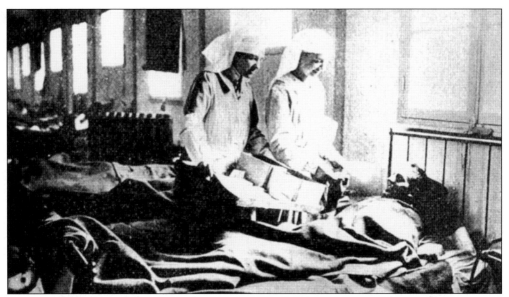

Susan Ryerson went on to become a bacteriologist during World War I. As action closed in on the field hospital where she was working, she stayed until the wounded were evacuated. For her heroism, she received the Croix De Guerre and the Medaille de la Reconnaissance. During the war, she met George Patterson, an American officer serving in France who was also a recipient of the Croix De Guerre. She married him in Paris in 1918. (Courtesy Minisink Valley Historical Society.)

Returning home after the war, Susan Patterson became active in the affairs of the Morristown community where the couple lived. She was involved with the Morristown Orchestral Society and Housing Committee of the Civic Society. She died childless in 1921 and is buried in the Lakeside Cemetery in Cooperstown, New York. Her husband, George Patterson, who was editor of the Morris County newspaper the *Jerseyman*, died in 1925. (Courtesy Judy Beckwith.)

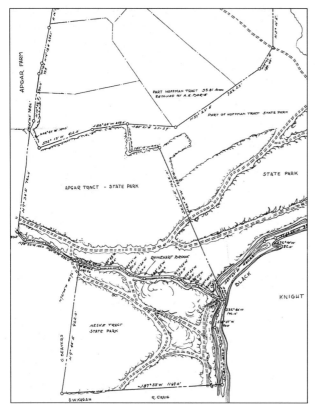

In 1929, Adolphe Borie donated an additional 90 acres, which extended the park to more than 120 acres. Almost immediately after that, Borie suggested to the state that he might be willing to donate even more land to the park. As part of his vision for the park, Borie suggested a new entrance into the park, farther south along the Black River. (Courtesy Voorhees State Park.)

A second entrance was constructed at the southwestern end of the park boundary, on a road that ran parallel with the Black River and then out to Black River Road. The beautiful gateway overlooking the river was also paid for by Adolphe Borie. This was the only other entrance visitors could use at the time, although it was more difficult to access. (Courtesy Voorhees State Park.)

With the acceptance of the donation, the state legislature authorized funding for developing and maintaining the park. The state improved the trails and built fireplaces, picnic areas, comfort stations, bridges, benches, and several shelters. Most of those features of the 1920s were located on the existing trail and road network and are now gone. Remnants, however, including this foundation of a comfort station, can still be found. (Courtesy Voorhees State Park.)

At least three rain shelters, as they were called, likely were built prior to 1933. The foundations can still be found, including this one at the junction of the Wintershine and Lower Trails, near the former main entrance into the park. (Courtesy Voorhees State Park.)

It is believed that the first superintendent of Hacklebarney State Park was C. E. Pollock, whose official title was park guard. He lived in the mill tender's house, at the park's entrance, and served through the CCC era and into the 1940s. Pollock alone managed the more than 20,000 individuals who visited the park annually. Even though access and publicity were limited, visitors came from New York City, Morristown, and nearby communities. Pictured here is park visitor Albert Kay and a 1924 Model T Ford. Kay and his wife, Elizabeth, later donated acreage in Chester that became the Kay Environmental Center. (Courtesy Chester Historical Society.)

One of the few surviving pre-CCC-era buildings associated with the park is the concession stand operated by Mahlon and Elizabeth Pitney. The structure was originally moved from the Hacklebarney Farm Cider Mill to the small parking area at the park's entrance. When the new visitor center opened, the building was moved back to the farm. The state no longer owns the former parking area. (Courtesy Voorhees State Park.)

# Two
# VOORHEES STATE PARK
## A GOVERNOR'S VISION

The land that now encompasses Voorhees State Park is part of a rolling landscape that existed for almost 200 years as a rural, agricultural region. The area, now overgrown by trees in most places, belies the fact that the park was once a working farm with pastures, an orchard, wood lot, and farm service buildings, along with a large home. The farm was operated until 1927.

Like Hacklebarney, Voorhees State Park is the result of the generosity of a visionary, in this case Foster McGowan Voorhees (1856–1927), whose family had lived in Hunterdon County for many years. Voorhees was an important figure in the state's history, as he was appointed acting governor in 1898 and was considered a "war governor" because the Spanish-American War was fought during his term. Camp Voorhees was established at Sea Girt, and all four regiments of the volunteers who came from New Jersey to fight in the war were mustered there.

Due to a constitutional limitation, Voorhees resigned as acting governor and then ran for governor and was elected in a close race in 1898. He served from 1899 to 1902. His accomplishments include investigations into several scandals, establishment of the first state budget, better treatment for the poor and unfortunate, the opening of the Rahway Reformatory for less-hardened criminals, educational reform, and mosquito control in the Meadowlands. In 1900, along with New York Gov. Theodore Roosevelt, Voorhees signed legislation creating the Palisades Interstate Park Commission, which allowed for the preservation of the Palisades along the Hudson River.

Foster McGowan Voorhees descended from a family with a long and distinguished role in the nation's history. The Voorhees surname has been modified over the last three centuries to include a range of interpretations, from Van Voorhees to Vorys. The family originated from Voor Hees in the Drenthe Province of the Netherlands. (Reprinted from *Northwestern New Jersey: A History of Somerset, Morris, Hunterdon, Warren and Sussex*.)

Foster Voorhees, the first child of Nathaniel and Naomi (Leigh) Voorhees, was born on November 5, 1856, in Clinton, just south of the location that later became Voorhees State Park. His father was a lawyer and banker and was active in political affairs. His maternal grandparents, Mary and Samuel Leigh, lived with the family. He had three brothers (Samuel, Nathaniel, and Edwin) and two sisters (Mary and Elizabeth). (Courtesy Nancy Conod and Nancy Vocci.)

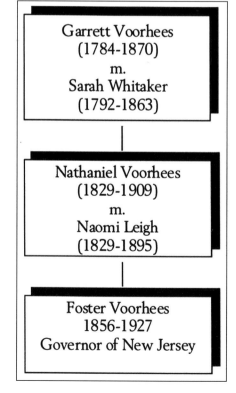

Garrett Voorhees
(1784-1870)
m.
Sarah Whitaker
(1792-1863)

Nathaniel Voorhees
(1829-1909)
m.
Naomi Leigh
(1829-1895)

Foster Voorhees
1856-1927
Governor of New Jersey

Foster Voorhees grew up in this Italianate house located at 69 Center Street in Clinton. Both of his sisters continued to live in the house until their deaths, and the house is still lovingly maintained to this day. As a young man, Voorhees went to Rutgers College, receiving his B.A. in 1876. After graduation, he taught foreign languages in the Rutgers Grammar School and, later, became a trustee of Rutgers University. (Courtesy Voorhees State Park.)

**Gov. Foster M. Voorhees**

In 1878, Voorhees moved to Elizabeth, where he studied law and, in 1880, established a law practice. His law offices were located at 142 Broad Street, and his home was at 297 North Broad Street. He was elected to the Elizabeth Board of Education and then as a Republican state assemblyman (1889–1890) and state senator from Union County (1894–1898). He served as president of the state senate in 1898. (Courtesy Voorhees State Park.)

Members of the Voorhees family were active philanthropists in the community and attended the Clinton Presbyterian Church, a short walk from their home on Center Street. Foster Voorhees split his time between Elizabeth and High Bridge and was a member of the Westminister Presbyterian Church in Elizabeth. When at High Bridge, he attended the High Bridge Reformed Church. (Courtesy Voorhees State Park.)

In the early years of the 20th century, the Voorhees family held several reunions, including this one on July 11, 1905, in Clinton. Foster Voorhees is pictured at the far right. One of the results of these gatherings was the creation of a family association dedicated to the preservation of the family's history. (Courtesy Voorhees State Park.)

In 1906, Foster Voorhees purchased a small stone house and its surrounding 323-acre farm known as Hill Acres, on present-day Hunterdon County Route 513, two miles north of High Bridge. Additions were built on both ends of the house during Voorhees's lifetime, giving the building its current configuration. It is believed that Voorhees planted the trees in front of the house, which have obscured the building from view. (Courtesy Voorhees State Park.)

Foster Voorhees came to High Bridge on weekends so that he could attend to local business and family affairs. This room, part of a 1918 addition to the building, was his library. Ralph Voorhees, whose grandfather was a cousin of the governor, visited the mansion in the 1930s and 1940s. Here, he stands beside one of the bookcases. (Courtesy Voorhees State Park.)

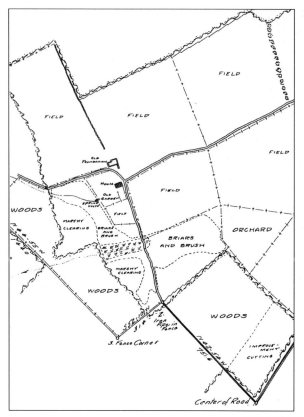

Hill Acres was a working farm, and Foster Voorhees loved to walk the property and took an active role in managing it. Acreage was dedicated to wood lots, chickens, orchards, and fields for wheat, rye, and hay. Today, the former farm is unrecognizable, completely overgrown with trees. The house shown in the center was probably the manager's and was located near the current Hoppock Picnic Grove. (Courtesy Voorhees State Park.)

After his retirement, the former governor continued to practice law. He never married, and he lived at his home until his death, which occurred on June 14, 1927, after several years of ill health. He was buried in the family plot at the Riverside Cemetery, adjacent to the Clinton Presbyterian Church, and his farm was donated to the state to use for forestry demonstration projects. (Courtesy Voorhees State Park.)

Once the state took control of the property, James Ashey was given the responsibility of managing it. He is probably the most important state official associated with the park. Having come from Washington Crossing State Park in 1930, he was instrumental in developing the vision of what the park is today. Ashey, pictured here, was the superintendent from 1930 through 1941. (Courtesy James Ashey Jr.)

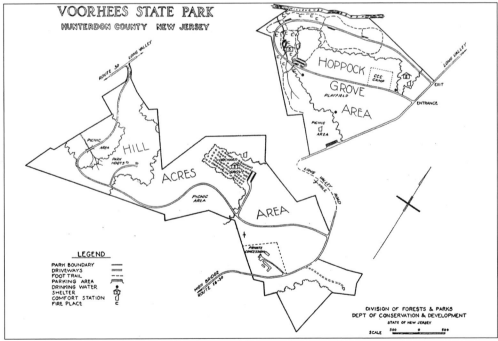

This map from the 1930s shows how the park was created from two separate tracts. The southern parcel was called the Hill Acres Tract, and the northern parcel was called the Hoppock Tract. James Ashey probably laid out the plans for the park's future use after the Voorhees donation. He later served as superintendent of Parvin State Park in Pittsgrove Township. (Courtesy Voorhees State Park.)

As funding allowed, former farm roads were improved and trails were constructed. During the early 1930s, the state built picnic tables, picnic groves, fireplaces, water supplies, and sanitary facilities and placed them in the parts of the park that were accessible to the public. (Courtesy Chester Barwick.)

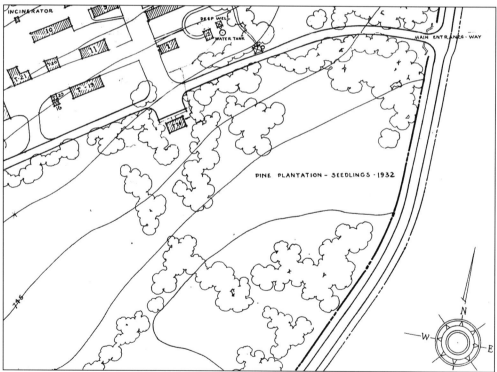

Early on, the state began planting experimental and specimen tree plantations on both tracts and undertook improvement cuttings. Even Gov. Foster Voorhees had created a plantation prior to his death. Several red pine plantations were planted in 1932, the first step toward fulfilling the governor's wishes that the park be used as a forestry demonstration park. Today, the trees have grown to maturity. (Courtesy Voorhees State Park.)

# *Three*

# WE CAN TAKE IT!
## THE ARRIVAL OF THE CCC

Against the backdrop of America on the move, enjoying its newly created national and state parks and forests, the economic calamity known as the Great Depression descended upon the nation and lasted from 1929 to 1941. Thousands of banks collapsed, and with that, fortunes and savings accounts disappeared. The stock market collapsed, and the country witnessed unprecedented poverty and unemployment. The nation's forests and farms had been devastated by years of bad management practices. Huge clouds of dust rolled east from the Midwest and Great Plains, causing the decade to become known as the "Dirty Thirties."

In the presidential election of 1932, Pres. Herbert Hoover was soundly defeated by New York Gov. Franklin D. Roosevelt, who called for a "New Deal" for the people. As part of that program, Roosevelt created a civilian conservation corps when he came into office. In March 1933, he had his cabinet draw up plans to put young men to work in the parks and forests of the country.

By June 1933, the Civilian Conservation Corps had been created by an act entitled "Emergency Conservation Work." For the first time in American history, four different cabinet agencies—the Departments of Labor, Interior, War, and Agriculture—all worked together on a program. As a group, these agencies managed the affairs of the CCC, along with its director, Robert Fechner, who coordinated the program. In the first year of the agency's existence, there were 22 camps in New Jersey and 4,000 young men enrolled. The cost to operate a typical CCC camp was about $180,000 a year.

Pres. Franklin D. Roosevelt's plan was to assist many of the millions of young men who were unemployed through no fault of their own. It is estimated that one quarter of the men aged 18 to 25 were unemployed during the Great Depression. The Depression affected young men no matter where they were from—farms, cities, or small towns. They became the cardinal concern of the CCC. (Reprinted from *We Can Take It: A Short Story of the CCC.*)

The administration of the camp at Voorhees, along with that of thousands of other CCC camps, was a collaborative effort between the U.S. Department of Labor, the War Department (U.S. Army) and, in the case of state or national parks, the National Park Service, the U.S. Department of the Interior, and the park superintendent. Pictured here is an illustration from a camp newsletter, showing how the arrangement worked. (Courtesy Center for Research Libraries Collection.)

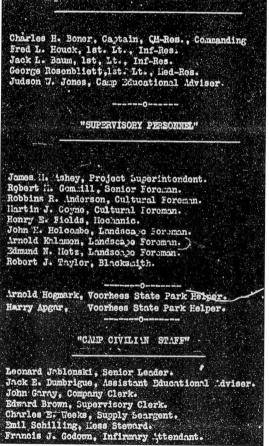

"ADVISORY STAFF"

Charles H. Boner, Captain, QM-Res., Commanding
Fred L. Houck, 1st. Lt., Inf-Res.
Jack L. Baum, 1st. Lt., Inf-Res.
George Rosenbliett, 1st. Lt., Med-Res.
Judson J. Jones, Camp Educational Adviser.

-----o-----

"SUPERVISORY PERSONNEL"

James H. Ashey, Project Superintendent.
Robert M. Gommill, Senior Foreman.
Robbins R. Anderson, Cultural Foreman.
Martin J. Coyne, Cultural Foreman.
Henry E. Fields, Mechanic.
John M. Holcombe, Landscape Foreman.
Arnold Kalamon, Landscape Foreman.
Edmund N. Hotz, Landscape Foreman.
Robert J. Taylor, Blacksmith.

-----o-----

Arnold Hogmark, Voorhees State Park Helper.
Harry Apgar, Voorhees State Park Helper.

-----o-----

"CAMP CIVILIAN STAFF"

Leonard Jablonski, Senior Leader.
Jack E. Dumbrigue, Assistant Educational Adviser.
John Garay, Company Clerk.
Edward Brown, Supervisory Clerk.
Charles E. Weeks, Supply Seargent.
Emil Schilling, Mess Steward.
Francis J. Godown, Infirmary Attendant.

The U.S. Army ran all of the CCC camps, overseeing sanitation, food, maintenance, discipline, and payroll. The army also took care of transportation needs. The National Park Service was responsible for work projects and for the men's activities during the day. Pictured here is Captain Rosen, one of the military commanders stationed at Voorhees over the years. (Courtesy Joseph Richardson.)

Capt. Charles Boner, another commander, and his wife, Terry, are pictured here standing in front of the officers' quarters with Rags, the company mascot, in 1936. Throughout the years, the turnover of the military was fairly regular. The army tried to expose as many of its officers as possible to the management of camps, as it was believed to be helpful to the officer corps. (Courtesy Chester Barwick.)

James Ashey (right) appears to have served the dual role of National Park Service work project superintendent and state park superintendent. He was responsible for overseeing the CCC efforts and projects done on behalf of the state. He was succeeded by Alan Blackman. Pictured with him is Martin Coyne, another National Park Service foreman. Project superintendents were paid $225 per month. (Courtesy Chester Barwick.)

Robbins Anderson is described as the "civilian administrator," on the back of this photograph. More accurately, he was the cultural foreman who worked for the National Park Service and was responsible for oversight of the various work projects. Foremen received between $150 to $170 per month and came from all walks of life. Some were college graduates, and others were master craftsmen. (Courtesy Joseph Richardson.)

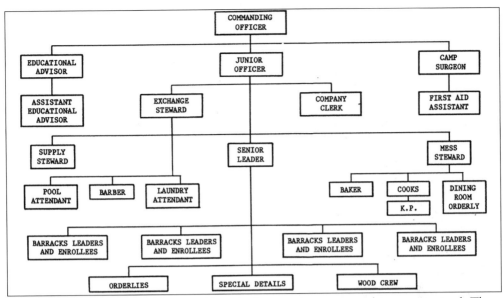

Each CCC company had 200 men, although that number was not always maintained. There were four kinds of companies: junior enrollees, World War I veterans, African Americans, and Native Americans (who worked on their own reservations). Pictured here is the organizational chart for a typical CCC company. Each man was ranked, and leadership was developed from within the ranks. (Courtesy National Archives Records Administration, 35-12, 9.)

To signify their rank or position, CCC boys wore patches on their uniform. Pictured here, clockwise from the upper left, are a set of chevrons worn by ranked men and cook, library, and quartermaster patches. In the center is a general organizational patch. Another layer of leadership came from the so-called "LEMs," the local experienced men, who were skilled at working outdoors and helped the enrollees adapt to their new situation. (Courtesy Doug Kiovsky.)

June 8, 1934

The CCC camp at Voorhees was initially known as Camp No. 20, or Camp Voorhees. Later, it was given the designation of SP No. 5, with Company 1268 assigned to it. SP designated "state park," and the company number coincided with the Army Corps district. The men came from all over the state of New Jersey, although many were from the local area. On June 8, 1934, Company 1268 posed for this photograph on the parade grounds near the garages. (Courtesy Chester Barwick and Anthony Capizzi.)

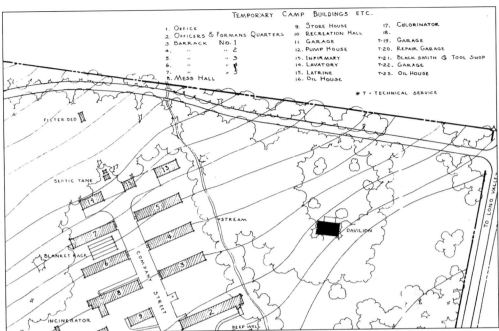

TEMPORARY CAMP BUILDINGS ETC.

1. OFFICE
2. OFFICERS & FORMANS QUARTERS
3. BARRACK No. 1
4. " " 2
5. " " 3
6. " " 4
7. " " 5
8. MESS HALL

9. STORE HOUSE
10. RECREATION HALL
11. GARAGE
12. PUMP HOUSE
13. INFIRMARY
14. LAVATORY
15. LATRINE
16. OIL HOUSE

17. CHLORINATOR
18.
T-19. GARAGE
T-20. REPAIR GARAGE
T-21. BLACK SMITH & TOOL SHOP
T-22. GARAGE
T-23. OIL HOUSE

* T • TECHNICAL SERVICE

Each camp was concentrated in one location. On October 1, 1933, construction of the camp began. By October 15, 1933, the first enrollees began arriving from Priest River, Idaho, where they had been working in the national forests. By November 29, 1933, the camp was completed. This drawing illustrates what the camp looked like at the peak of its activity, in 1938, with 23 buildings. (Courtesy Voorhees State Park.)

This view is looking in a northerly direction up Company Street in 1934, with barracks on both sides. Enrollees improved the appearance of their barracks by creating walkways, chestnut guardrails, and stone borders and by maintaining the buildings. Locals gave flower seeds to the camp to be used by the enrollees. Some of the stone borders can still be seen on Company Street. (Courtesy Mickey Nalence.)

A water fountain was located near the entrance of the CCC camp for the boys to use. Here, Brownie, a camp mascot, helps himself to some water. The camp had at least four other mascots during its lifetime, including Rags, Nellie, Mae, and Blackie. (Courtesy Chester Barwick.)

Army officers and National Park Service supervisors who were single or whose families were elsewhere lived full-time at the camp in the officers' quarters, shown here. Most officers and National Park Service supervisors lived in nearby towns such as Annandale, High Bridge, Clinton, Glen Gardner, and Califon. One, Robbins Anderson, was from Trenton and commuted home on weekends. (Courtesy Joseph Richardson.)

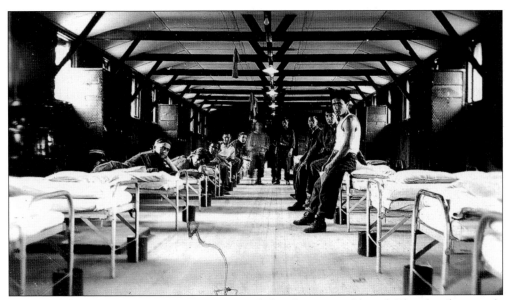

As part of their compensation, men were provided with room and board. They lived in simple buildings that housed 40 men and measured 20 feet by 112 feet. The barracks were heated by coal stoves, one of which is pictured on the left. Enrollee Joseph Richardson is lying on his bunk. An arrow points to him. (Courtesy Joseph Richardson.)

The office of the project superintendent was located at the entrance to the park, at the southern end of Company Street. Originally, a small building stood here, and then in 1939, the National Park Service built this larger structure, using local laborers. In this building, projects were designed and implemented and the camp's paperwork was stored. This was one of only two CCC camp buildings that survived the dismantling of the camp in 1945. (Courtesy Voorhees State Park.)

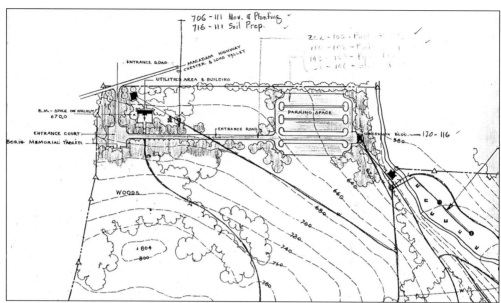

National Park Service foremen kept track of work projects with progress plans, which were given to regional and national offices for approval. Here, the notations describe the project number, and the shading indicates where work was being completed at Hacklebarney State Park. (Courtesy Voorhees State Park.)

The National Park Service provided the heavy equipment necessary to undertake the building of the roads and structures. At one point, there were a 1.5-ton pickup, two stake body trucks, and four 1.5-ton dump trucks on site. Pictured here is one the dump trucks with "National Park Service" emblazoned on its door. Technical services trucks, used for both work and recreation activities for the boys, traveled 99,199 miles between 1933 and early 1936. (Courtesy Chester Barwick.)

After the initial organization of the CCC, the National Park Service was able to acquire heavy equipment for the various camps, which the CCC boys were trained to use. Here, a bulldozer, operated by an enrollee, levels an area. (Courtesy Albert Peterson Jr.)

Roadwork was made much easier in the mid-1930s, when the National Park Service brought in road graders like this. Camp Voorhees had its own gasoline pump and oil supply, which was located by the garages. There was also a repair and blacksmith shop for equipment and tools. (Courtesy Albert Peterson Jr.)

Enrollees gathered in front of the U.S. Department of Interior garages every morning at 8:00 a.m. to receive their work assignments and to get to the job sites, where they worked until 4:00 p.m. The men rode in open stake body trucks. Pictured here is the technical services garage, a short distance from the current park headquarters. (Courtesy Joseph Richardson.)

CIVILIAN CONSERVATION CORPS

P.C.   22677

**Proficiency**   **Certificate**

THIS IS TO CERTIFY THAT _____ Ernest Nixon

of _____ Mount Holly, New Jersey _____ while a member of C. C. C. Company _____ 1268 _____ of

_____ High Bridge, New Jersey _____ became proficient as _____ Truck Driver

Dated _____ March 30, 1940

Company Commander.

*Francis R. Bishop*
Camp Educational Adviser.

*Alan R. Black*
Project Superintendent.

Approved by the District Commander:

*Forrest G. Read*
District Educational Adviser.

U. S. GOVERNMENT PRINTING OFFICE      6—9673

A motor vehicle operator's permit was a valuable item for enrollees to obtain. Not only did it keep them from some of the more unpleasant chores in camp, like KP (kitchen police) duty, it was a valuable asset when they left the CCC and went back into the private sector. Many CCC boys went on to become truck drivers. Pictured here is Ernest Nixon's certificate for driving a truck. (Courtesy Ernest Nixon.)

## Four

# A DAY IN THE LIFE OF CCC COMPANY 1268

Although many former CCC boys describe life in camp as similar to being in the military, Pres. Franklin D. Roosevelt made sure that it was not and assured America of the same. The camps were run by army officers until the last year, but the men had much more freedom than they would have had in the regular army. They were not required to salute officers, nor did they have to go through any military training. The CCC provided room and board, health care, clothing, two weeks of vacation, and several holidays. When an enrollee's time was done, he was given transportation back to his hometown.

Most CCC boys remember both the excellent quality and quantity of the food. They adopted good lifelong eating habits after their stay at camp. The men also remember their nights out, when they pursued young ladies in the surrounding towns of High Bridge and Clinton and drank nickel beers in local bars willing to serve them. For many of the men, their time in the CCC was a great adventure.

To be sure, some did not like it, and they were usually gone in a short time. The majority of the enrollees, however, thought their experiences helped them get ready for a new life, in which they would return to their homes more mature, wiser, and with job training.

When a new enrollee came into a CCC camp, he was known as a rookie. Rookies were often subject to pranks played by the more experienced boys. Soon enough, however, the rookies were playing pranks on later newcomers. (Reprinted from *We Can Take It: A Short Story of the* CCC.)

Homesickness was a major problem in the CCC, and enrollees were encouraged to write home often. On one Mother's Day, the boys of Company 1268 were encouraged to write their mothers back home. Another problem was enrollees known as "the wise guys," men who left their barracks dirty or did not do as they were told. For them, KP duty was common. (Reprinted from *We Can Take It: A Short Story of the* CCC.)

Hearty and healthy food—much better than that served at many enrollees' impoverished homes—was served at CCC camps and, on average, an enrollee gained between 10 and 15 pounds. Pictured here is the exterior of Company 1268's mess hall, with the chow bell that was rung before meals. Breakfast and dinner were served here. A bulletin board told enrollees who had KP duty or fire watch and also gave other camp news. (Courtesy Michael Nalavany.)

Here, the cooking staff at Voorhees stands ready to serve up meals for hungry enrollees. Food was generally bought locally, partly to support the local economy and farmers. (Courtesy Chester Barwick.)

Lunch was usually served at the job site and eaten outdoors. If the weather was cold, a hot meal was served. Typically, however, lunch consisted of a sandwich, fruit, and something to drink. Enterprising lads would start a fire to toast their bread or warm their meals. (Courtesy Joseph Richardson.)

Medical care was available at all times and was provided at no charge. Only one enrollee, Leonard Birger, is believed to have died in the camp. He died in 1938, from a fever. A doctor was on call from High Bridge, and the infirmary was manned by a senior enrollee who handled minor medical problems. An ambulance, which also served the Hope, Raritan, and Hackettstown camps, was used for emergencies. (Courtesy Michael Nalavany.)

Medical care was excellent, and if an emergency occurred, CCC boys were sent to a medical facility in New York City. This postcard was sent to Albert Peterson in the Naval Hospital in Brooklyn from his friend JW. While humorous, it reflects the homesickness that some enrollees felt. "Bosco went over the hill already" means that Bosco had left the CCC and was absent without leave. (Courtesy Albert Peterson Jr.)

Howdy Pard,

I hope your feeling better now that you had your face—pardon, I meant abdomen—lifted. Its hard for me to get accustomed to this camp. The sociable, friendly spirit seems to be missing. You know what I mean. Bosco went over the hill already. Your friend

P.S. Drop me a card please.

Here, the camp's ambulance has been involved in a major accident, and we can guess that the driver, possibly a CCC enrollee, may have lost his driver's rating over this event. (Courtesy Mickey Nalence.)

Each CCC company usually had at least one member who would cut hair for a nickel. The men availed themselves of the service, and the barber enjoyed an extra source of income. CCC boys were paid $30 a month, and $25 was automatically sent home to family members or guardians for their support. The boys were paid their $5 share in biweekly allotments. (Courtesy Mickey Nalence.)

Personal appearance and physical well-being were important features of the CCC, and cleanliness was a hallmark. CCC boys had to do their own laundry, as we see Chester Barwick doing here in back of his barracks. Each man was assigned a bed and a footlocker, or a closet was provided. (Courtesy Chester Barwick.)

50

For many enrollees at Voorhees, the CCC provided vocational and avocational classes. The education program was known as the School of the Woods and included job training, current events, and access to a camp library. Academic subjects were taught in local schools, and guest lecturers came to the camp regularly, including some from Lafayette College in Easton. (Reprinted from *We Can Take It: A Short Story of the CCC*.)

CIVILIAN CONSERVATION CORPS

U. C.    39843

**Unit**  **Certificate**

THIS CERTIFIES THAT _____ Ernest B. Nixon _____ of Company ____ 1268 ____ has satisfactorily completed __ 13 __ hours of instruction in ____ Concrete Construction ____ and is therefore granted this Certificate.

_____                    _____
Project Superintendent.                      Company Commander.

_____
Camp Educational Adviser.

Date __ June 17, 1940 __     Place __ High Bridge, New Jersey __

ipo    6—9671

Ernest Nixon, an enrollee at Voorhees, attended a course in concrete construction and was the recipient of this certificate. Other courses included first aid and mechanical drawing. Since 45 percent of the men had never been employed and only 13 percent had graduated from high school, this education program was an important component of the CCC. (Courtesy Ernest Nixon.)

Many of the young men in the CCC had never done manual labor or worked with tools before their enlistment. By the time the boys left the CCC, they were proficient in the use of tools. Safety was an important concern of both the army and National Park Service, and regular instruction was given. (Courtesy Joseph Richardson.)

Photography was a popular hobby in CCC camps across the country, and there were even photography classes sponsored at Voorhees. With the introduction of inexpensive cameras and developing services, many enrollees took photographs during their time at Voorhees, and their pictures now form the basis for what we know about camp life. (Courtesy Jack Woollis.)

For camp news, enrollees turned to an in-house newsletter called the *State Parker*. In later years, it was called the *Voorhees Weekly*. This cover is typical of the newsletter, which was mimeographed and distributed to the boys. Even Barney Heckle contributed a regular piece about camp happenings. In addition to camp news, newsletters also provided moral guidance, practical work advice, and information on current events. (Courtesy Center for Research Libraries Collection.)

The quality of the *State Parker* received accolades from none other than Robert Fechner, the Washington-based director of the CCC, who wrote the camp in 1938, congratulating the boys on their newsletter. Fechner provided critical leadership to the CCC from 1933 until his death in 1939. (Courtesy Center for Research Libraries Collection.)

Radio was the medium of the day, and programs with Arthur Godfrey, Molly Goldberg, and Amos and Andy were popular, along with the movies that were shown in camp. There were Ping-Pong tables at the recreation hall, along with a pool table and a piano, which provided entertainment for the boys during their time off. The boys even made a trip to New York City to see the naval fleet during exercises in 1934. (Courtesy Chester Barwick.)

On Sunday, October 30, 1938, radio host Orson Welles narrated a program called *The War of the Worlds*. Many people across the nation, including thousands of men in hundreds of CCC camps, listened as the New York metropolitan area was destroyed by Martians. CCC boys at Voorhees thought, as did many others, that the Martians had really invaded. This company newsletter remembers the fear that some had. (Courtesy Center for Research Libraries Collection.)

54

On a day off, enrollee John Martin enjoys swimming in the falls at Lake Solitude in High Bridge. The CCC boys took advantage of the attractions at both parks and in the surrounding area. (Courtesy Chester Barwick.)

Responsible CCC boys could take a lifesaving course and then serve as lifeguards at public facilities, including those frequented by the CCC enrollees. At least one of the courses was held at High Point State Park. (Courtesy Chester Barwick.)

Boxing was a popular national sport in the 1930s, and most CCC camps, including the one at Voorhees, had a boxing team. Joseph Catania was a camp champion. Here, some of the enrollees from Company 1268 practice for an upcoming match. (Courtesy Chester Barwick.)

Baseball, basketball, softball, horseshoe pitching, and roller-skating were also popular activities. In addition, there were track meets and swimming competitions. Enrollees played intra-barracks, subdistrict, and local league games. (Reprinted from *We Can Take It: A Short Story of the CCC*.)

Occasionally, CCC boys displayed their sense of humor and mischievousness, as they did here by posing with a wooden Indian, borrowed from a local tobacco store. (Courtesy Mickey Nalence.)

Most CCC boys had a great sense of humor, as documented in this photograph. Safety, however, was an overriding concern in the CCC. Proper equipment was distributed, and safety instruction was regularly given. (Courtesy Mickey Nalence.)

For most area residents, their memories of CCC boys are of them arriving in the downtown business districts in an army truck like the one pictured here. The trucks were also sometimes used to transport young ladies to events held at the camp. (Courtesy Albert Peterson Jr.)

The CCC boys were allowed to leave the camp on their nights off. Two Company 1268 members are shown here in front of a store in High Bridge. In town, they shopped in local stores, ate in restaurants, and went to the movies. Enrollees drank nickel beers in local bars if they were of age or if the bartenders were willing to serve them. (Courtesy Mickey Nalence.)

Another popular activity was dancing, and many of Company 1268's members frequented a nearby dance hall on Route 31. The story goes that the woman whose face has been whited out was married and, therefore, did not want her picture taken. (Courtesy Joseph Richardson.)

The camp's administration encouraged the boys to put on shows to display their talents, and dance lessons were given for the boys in Easton. Other programs were sponsored by the local Kiwanis and by Ralph Space, from Space Farms in Sussex County, who brought a collection of rattlesnakes for display. There was also a camp orchestra. (Reprinted from *We Can Take It: A Short Story of the CCC*.)

Skiing became very popular in the 1930s, as did other winter sports. Here, one of the camp's officers, perhaps the camp's doctor, tries his hand at cross-country skiing. (Courtesy Chester Barwick.)

Most enrollees did not have cars and, in fact, were not allowed to have them. The ones that did have them, however, hid them in the woods on surrounding properties, or local farmers housed them in their barns. CCC boy Harry Eick is shown here in his first car after he got out of the CCC. (Courtesy Kathleen Daku.)

CCC boys often thought of and missed friends, girlfriends, home cooking, and use of the family car, or flivver, as it was known. Most had never been away from home for extended periods of time prior to their service in the CCC. (Courtesy Center for Research Libraries Collection.)

The young men often had pictures of women in their lockers and trunks. Here, Eugene Nalence (left) and his friend Tony admire a starlet of the time. Some parents forbade their daughters from dating CCC boys because they had no idea where the boys came from or what their backgrounds were like. (Courtesy Mickey Nalence.)

One of the results of the interaction between the CCC boys and local girls was the inevitable CCC marriage. Harry F. Eick was still in the CCC when he met Margaret Ansbach at a dance sponsored by one of the local dance halls. After his service in the CCC, the couple married on April 21, 1935. Margaret's brother Ralph Ansbach was also in the CCC at Voorhees. (Courtesy Kathleen Daku.)

Like so many from the Great Depression generation, Margaret and Harry Eick remained married until he died in 1970. This photograph was taken in 1967. (Courtesy Kathleen Daku.)

NO "GOLDBRICKING" HERE

Some enrollees who shirked their duties were known as "goldbrickers." As a penalty, they were assigned some of the more unpleasant tasks in camp. If a boy left the CCC without permission, it was said that he had "gone over the hill." If he served his full term, he was given an honorable discharge. (Reprinted from *We Can Take It: A Short Story of the CCC*.)

Some CCC boys hoped to go west to Idaho or Montana but were stationed only a short distance from home. No matter their location, most CCC boys acquired, if they did not already have it, a great love of the outdoors. In the decades that followed their work in the camps, many of them became great advocates for the parks and urged that the parks be maintained and adequately funded. (Courtesy Mickey Nalence.)

Possibly as many as 1,000 men served at Voorhees between 1933 and 1941. An average enrollee spent nine months in the CCC, but some spent as long as two years, the maximum allowed. Enrollees who were experienced and rated, or ranked, sometimes stayed longer. Occasionally, small groups of men were sent off in cadres to open new camps. Most of the young men left the CCC in much better shape than when they arrived. The outdoor life, good food, and hard work made better men of them, and in many cases prepared them for an uncertain world, soon to become embroiled in World War II. Pictured in June 1934 is the gang that built Hill Acres Road. From left to right are the following: (first row) Lew Gomlock, Anthony Capizzi, H. D. Rivers, and John Robinski; (second row) Ed Braden, Stan Bobinski, Mike Spiati, Jim Deitrich, Joe Baer, Howard Cella, Elmer Perrien, Ken Biggs, Bob Dorland, Howard Freela, and Eugene Nalence. (Courtesy Mickey Nalence.)

*Five*

# THE CCC WORK PROJECTS AT VOORHEES STATE PARK

When the CCC arrived at Voorhees, most of the park was not accessible to the public because of a lack of good roads and facilities. The park still reflected Gov. Foster Voorhees's use of the property as a farm, with pastures, woodland, barns, and an apple orchard. One of the first priorities of the National Park Service managers was to create access to all of the property facilities that the public could use, aside from what had already been done in the years preceding the arrival of the CCC.

As the CCC boys began work in the summer of 1933, they found a farm that would be transformed into a park. By 1941, when the camp closed, most of the park was open to the public, with new touring roads, truck trails, hiking trails, pavilions, picnic tables, parking areas, and a scenic overlook. It had been transformed into a multiuse facility.

Upon arriving at Voorhees, National Park Service designers, working for what was called the technical services, created master plans for the development of both Voorhees and Hacklebarney. This legend, from one of the two master plans created for Voorhees, demonstrates the cooperative nature of the relationship between the National Park Service and Division of Forests and Parks, as represented by C. B. Wilber and National Park Service senior foreman Robert Gemmill. (Courtesy Voorhees State Park.)

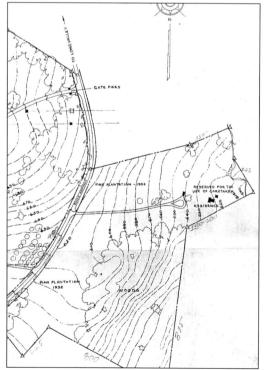

A survey of a park's boundary was always a top priority for the National Park Service because the federal government did not want to spend money improving private property. The triangles indicate where boundary markers were later installed. (Courtesy Voorhees State Park.)

The park's boundary line was designated with concrete markers like this one with a dial inserted at the top. This monument is probably from the original survey after the Voorhees donation. Most of the markers remain in the park. Some can still be seen but are now inside the current boundaries due to subsequent land acquisitions, which enlarged the park. (Courtesy Voorhees State Park.)

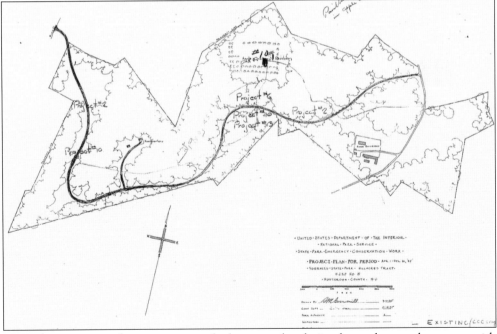

First, planners created an inventory of what was already in the park, or a base map with elevations and boundaries. From that base map came the master plan, complete with roads, utilities, lakes, streams, and proposed projects. (Courtesy Voorhees State Park.)

A hand-carved wood park entrance sign stood at the entrance to the park on Route 513 and announced that visitors had arrived at the home of Company 1268. (Courtesy Michael Nalavany.)

One of the first projects undertaken was the 1934 construction of a large, handsome stone gateway at the main entrance of the park. As part of construction of the gateway, two handsome cast-iron plaques were installed. They could be seen from either direction on the road. One reads "Voorhees State Park," and the other reads "Hoppock Grove." (Courtesy Mickey Nalence.)

During the early years at Voorhees, road gangs opened the interior of the park by building new roads or improving existing farm roads. After a survey crew laid out the route, road gangs came in to build it. Survey stakes can be seen here along High Acres Road (now known as Hill Acres Road) near the current site of the New Jersey Astronomical Association's observatory. (Courtesy Mickey Nalence.)

Road building throughout the park required moving tons of rock and providing a finished surface for automobiles. Large amounts of dynamite were used to blast rock. It took several years to build Hill Acres Road. Here, Joe Bauer and Howard Cella excavate a rock from the future roadbed in the summer of 1934. From this hard work came the CCC's motto, "We Can Take It!" (Courtesy Mickey Nalence.)

A large stone crusher was used to create fill for road projects, and this photograph was probably taken along Hill Acres Road. This piece of equipment, created by the CCC boys, was featured in the national CCC newspaper, *Happy Days*. One enrollee remembered that it took three efforts at creating the bend in Hill Acres Road near Buffalo Hollow Road before the bend met the standard. (Courtesy Chester Barwick.)

The roadwork at Voorhees moved thousands of tons of rock and required heavy-duty machinery. At one point the rock-handling crew was crushing 100 tons of rock a day. While the roads have been improved in the years since their construction, the basic layouts and sizes remain the same. (Courtesy Albert Peterson Jr.)

Enrollees dressed, or finished, the road and its shoulders. The surface would ultimately be blacktopped by the state. Where there once were either no roads or only rugged farm roads, there were now finished roads, ready for touring cars. State Park Road (then known as Hoppock Grove Road) was 1.1 miles long and 18 feet wide. It took 68,250 man-hours to build and required 2,320 tons of ballast rock and 4,500 tons of crushed rock to complete. (Courtesy Chester Barwick.)

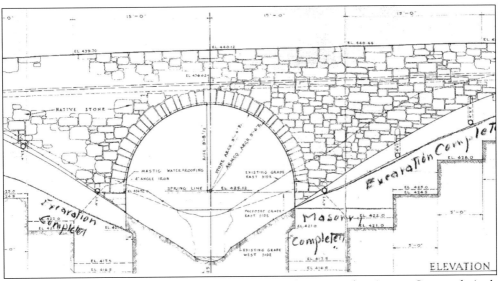

One of the most significant structures built at Voorhees was the Armco Sectional Arch Vehicular Bridge, on the Hill Acres Tract, which crossed a stream near Buffalo Hollow Road. This bridge still survives. With its use of hand-cut stone creating a rustic look, this bridge shows the typical hallmarks of National Park Service designs. (Courtesy Voorhees State Park.)

The CCC boys, under the supervision of National Park Service foremen, found the stone in the surrounding area, cut and shaped it, installed the corrugated sectional arch, laid the stone, and finished off the entranceways. This picture may be of the construction of the Hoppock Bridge. The rail in the foreground was laid to deliver the stone and concrete to the lowest levels of the foundation. (Courtesy Albert Peterson Jr.)

Six new parking areas were created in Voorhees at various convenient places along Hill Acres Road and State Park Road in order to accommodate the growing number of visitors. All used large boulders that were found during road construction. Culverts were also built by the CCC boys for road drainage, and more than 3,000 feet of guardrails were installed. (Courtesy Voorhees State Park.)

72

The CCC also created a scenic overlook, which is still used by park visitors today. Many tons of fill were brought here to create the promontory. The view during the 1930s was of "the Valley," as it was known then. Today, visitors look across the Round Valley Recreation Area, which was built in 1977. More fill has been added to enlarge the area. (Courtesy Mickey Nalence.)

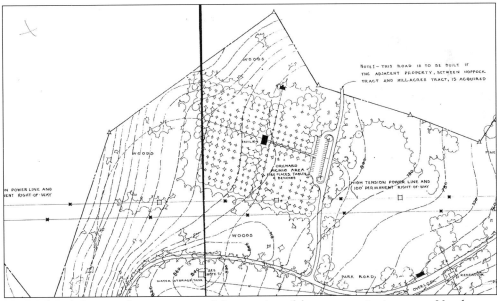

National Park Service planners proposed the creation of three group picnic areas at Voorhees—one on the Hill Acres Tract and two on the Hoppock Tract. The Orchard Picnic Area, on Hill Acres Road, was built in 1934 and was located in the governor's apple orchard, where visitors could pick apples while picnicking. National Park Service planners presumed that the park would expand to connect the Hoppock and Hill Acres Tracts. (Courtesy Voorhees State Park.)

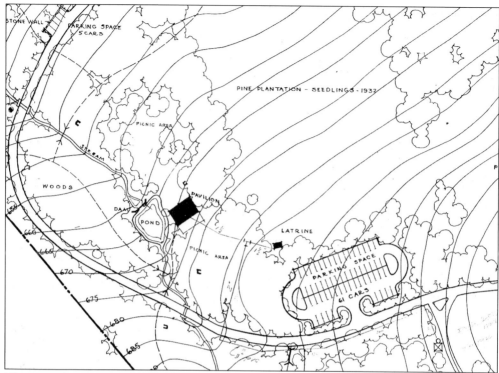

The second group picnic area was located in the Hoppock Tract and was one of the most impressive projects that the CCC boys accomplished at Voorhees. A new pond and several bridges were created, along with a beautiful stone retaining wall. The third picnic area was created directly across from the current park office. (Courtesy Voorhees State Park.)

Here, a CCC boy works on one of the three pavilions, probably at the Orchard Picnic Area. The use of large timbers and stone is a hallmark of the style of design that has come to be known as "parkitecture." Included in the picnic areas were tables, fireplaces, comfort stations, and water facilities. In all, more than 30 picnic table combinations were built by the boys. (Courtesy Voorhees State Park.)

Among the most impressive projects built by the CCC boys at Voorhees were the timber-framed picnic shelters at the three group picnic areas. Designs used at Voorhees and all of the CCC camps were usually generated at a local level, although generic designs were also provided by the National Park Service Branch of Plans and Design. The plans for the picnic pavilions at Voorhees were of such a high quality that they were featured in the 1938 *Parks and Recreation Structures* style book, published by the National Park Service. Each pavilion cost $640 in materials to build. (Above, reprinted from Parks and Recreation Structures, courtesy Doug Kiovsky; below, courtesy Voorhees State Park.)

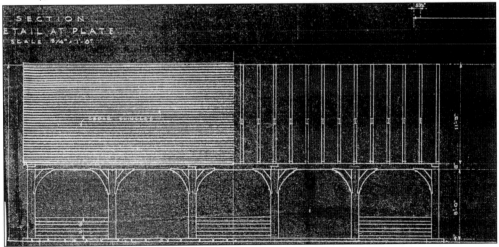

After the Voorhees Family Association was organized in 1932, a reunion was held at Voorhees State Park. The group made use of one of the pavilions that had recently been built by the CCC. (Courtesy Ralph Voorhees.)

Much of the labor required of the CCC boys was hard and physically demanding. Trail construction in both parks required moving rock and providing a stable hiking surface. The boys took great pride in the finished roads and trails they built at Voorhees and Hacklebarney. (Courtesy Joseph Richardson.)

The enrollees repaired damaged trees, cleared out dead trees, and removed brush to eliminate forest fire hazards. They also thinned out forests and cut up deadwood. Several hundred trees, along with shrubs, were planted at Voorhees by the CCC boys. Now, 70 years later, those trees have grown to maturity. As a company newsletter said, "Every tree planted will last longer than the life of the man who planted them." (Courtesy Chester Barwick.)

The enrollees wore out lots of equipment, including shovels, picks, and bars. Here, enrollees are probably clearing brush and dismantling some of the farm features on the former Hill Acres farm. Even as the CCC boys were working in the park, visitors began to use the facilities as soon as they became available. (Courtesy Chester Barwick.)

There were many other projects completed by the CCC in order to enhance park operations and to maintain the CCC camp. Here, a CCC crew lays a clay tile sewer line somewhere in Voorhees. It is not known whether this was repair work to the CCC sanitary facilities or a new installation. The boys also razed a large barn in close proximity to the Voorhees mansion. (Courtesy Joseph Richardson.)

CCC boys also assisted with game feeding and building shelters at Voorhees State Park, where they raised and released 75 pheasant chicks into the park. Company 1268 boys worked at the Clinton Wildlife Management Area, planting trees and shrubs and working on fence lines and stream improvement. They also worked at the New Jersey Fish and Game Preserve in Union, helping with roads and plantings. (Courtesy Chester Barwick.)

Other off-site projects included work at the New Jersey Tuberculosis Sanatorium at Mount Kipp. Located in Glen Gardner, about four miles from Voorhees, the hospital is now known as the Senator Garrett W. Haggadorn Geriatric Psychiatric Hospital. The building can be seen in the center distance. The CCC boys planted 130,000 spruce and red pine seedlings around the property. (Courtesy Voorhees State Park.)

While working at Mount Kipp, the CCC boys also cleared and burned brush. After working with the rock crusher on park roads, one newsletter writer said, "We're the dust eaters from the CCC—We'll soon be in Glen Gardner with the old TB." The CCC also helped with other emergency projects, like firefighting and snow removal. (Courtesy Albert Peterson Jr.)

On June 30, 1941, Company 1268 closed its doors. There was discussion, first, of using the camp as a retreat for British naval personnel, and then, as a headquarters for the Women's Auxiliary Corps, because of its proximity to the Philadelphia shipyards. Neither proposal came to fruition. In March 1945, with the CCC buildings deteriorating from a lack of maintenance, a local contractor removed the remaining 19 wooden buildings for $3,005. This aerial view, taken during the 1960s, shows the work project superintendent's office on the left and the CCC barn at the top center. (Courtesy Voorhees State Park.)

There were only two buildings left standing from the original CCC camp—the technical services garage and the project superintendent's office. Today, the garage is used for storage purposes. After the CCC camp closed, the office was used as a home for the park's superintendents until it was demolished in 1993. (Courtesy Voorhees State Park.)

The chimney of the officers' and technical service quarters still stands. Along with the foundations of several other buildings, this is one of the few structural remnants of the camp. Visitors can still see evidence of where the buildings stood, however, and building footprints have recently been created by park staff. (Courtesy Voorhees State Park.)

During the CCC era, the park's headquarters were located in the Hill Acres Tract, near where the current maintenance building is located. The building on the left, which has since been demolished, was the park headquarters. (Courtesy Voorhees State Park.)

*Six*

# THE CCC WORK PROJECTS AT HACKLEBARNEY STATE PARK

In 1935, even as major work was being completed at Voorhees, efforts began at Hacklebarney, building on the considerable work that had been done by the state following the Borie donations. The park's entrance was moved from the northeastern corner to the northwestern corner of the property. A new road, an entrance court and plaza, a contact station and concession stand, a shop and storage building, and trails were all constructed by the CCC, along with a water distribution system.

In 1938, most of the CCC work force was shifted to Hacklebarney. One newsletter writer later wrote, "The men of SP-5 can feel a sense of pride as they view the present work at Hacklebarney drawing to a state of completion." By June 30, 1941, when Company 1268 was shut down, most of the conservation and forestry projects were completed at both parks, and with that, its mission was accomplished. The forests within both park boundaries were in good health again, and the properties were more accessible to the public. The CCC left $6,000 worth of materials behind to help the state complete the remaining proposed projects. The success of companies like 1268 earned the CCC one of its best-known nicknames, the "Roosevelt Tree Army."

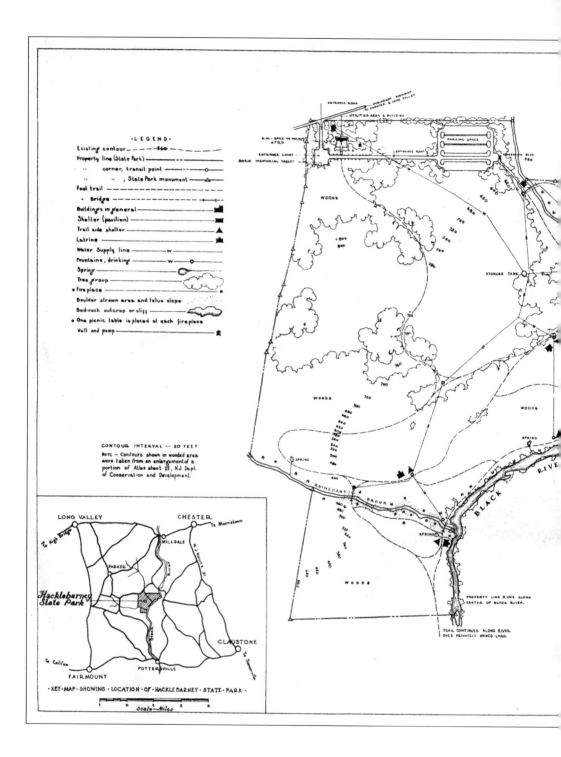

·LEGEND·

Existing contour __ __ __ __ 860
Property line (State Park) _____
  "    corner, transit point _____⊙
  "    " , State Park monument _____△
Foot trail __ __ __ __ __ __
  · bridge __ __ __ __ __ __⟩⟨
Buildings in general _____⬛
Shelter (pavilion) _____⬛
Trail side shelter _____▲
Latrine _____⬛
Water Supply line _____w
Fountains, drinking _____w
Spring _____
Tree group _____
· fire place _____ᴀ
Boulder strewn area and talus slope ∴∴∴
Bed-rock outcrop or cliff _____
· One picnic table is placed at each fireplace
Well and pump _____

CONTOUR INTERVAL — 20 FEET

Note — Contours shown in wooded area
were taken from an enlargement of a
portion of Atlas sheet 23, N.J. Dept
of Conservation and Development.

Hacklebarney
State Park

·KEY·MAP·SHOWING·LOCATION·OF·HACKLEBARNEY·STATE·PARK·

Scale~Miles

84

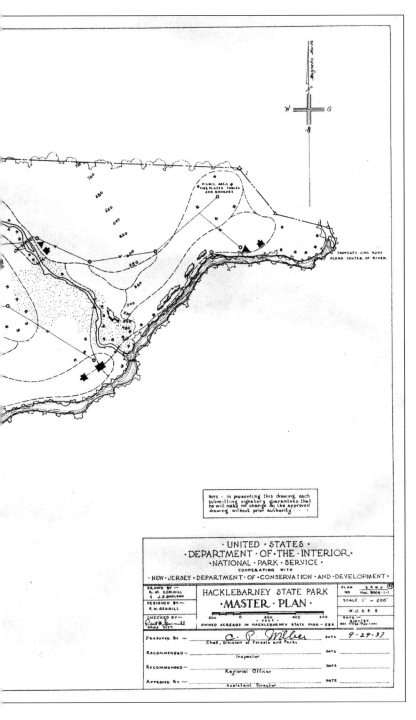

As in all CCC projects, properties were developed to look and operate like national parks, giving them a consistent appearance across the country. In the case of Hacklebarney, National Park Service designers made the decision in 1933 to move the park's entrance, the result of discussions the state had been having with Adolphe Borie since 1931. Borie proposed donating, and then donated, an additional 55 acres in 1935. (Courtesy Voorhees State Park.)

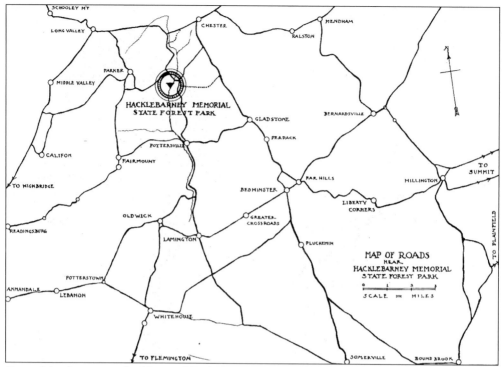

One of the first issues the National Park Service considered in 1933 was how the public could better access and use Hacklebarney. With Adolphe Borie's donation in 1935 and the addition of another sliver of land, access to the proposed new county road that would pass the park entrance was obtained. There were a number of farm buildings on the newly acquired property, near the current entrance, which were subsequently demolished. (Courtesy Voorhees State Park.)

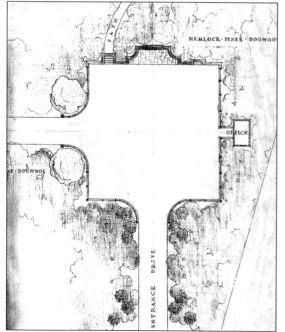

With these new acquisitions, National Park Service designers could plan a new entrance that was almost identical in design to the original. One of the handsomest CCC features designed for the park, the entrance plaza, was drawn by Robert Gemmill. Some of the features that were not built included a park office and the entrance to a trail to Lookout Hill. When the new park entrance was completed, the old one was eliminated. (Courtesy Voorhees State Park.)

The two small bronze plaques were removed from the old entrance, along with the large memorial plaque, and mounted on cut stone features at the center of the plaza. A cut stone bench sits below the main plaque. Park history has is that the masons put their pictures in a jar that they then placed in the space behind the plaque. (Courtesy Voorhees State Park.)

Part of the rationale for the new entrance was that it would create better access and parking for the growing number of visitors, which in 1932 was estimated at 66,732 people. It was the single most expensive project that the CCC built, costing $49,238. The cedar trees that now line the road into the parking lot and surround the area were planted by the CCC boys, along with shrubs and trees. (Courtesy Voorhees State Park.)

The new entrance eliminated the former inconvenient right of way at the end of a narrow dirt road, which was a short distance from the Borie residence. After the stone pillars and tablets were removed, the old right of way into the park was sold back to Adolphe Borie in 1935. It is now overgrown and unrecognizable except to longtime residents and park historians. (Courtesy Voorhees State Park.)

Even as projects were going on at Voorhees, CCC work gangs were transported to Hacklebarney. Each day, army trucks rumbled out of the camp, heading toward the sister park, some 16 miles away. Here, boys wait on line for their lunch meal. (Courtesy Mickey Nalence.)

By 1935, a CCC crew was removing underbrush and thinning and cutting dead trees for use as split rails, telephone poles, lumber, and firewood. Hundreds of truckloads of brush were burned, eliminating a major fire hazard. (Courtesy Jack Woollis.)

All across Hacklebarney, red pine seedlings were planted, and today they are mature trees. They are usually recognizable because they are planted in symmetrical rows equidistant from each other. (Courtesy Voorhees State Park.)

Known in the CCC-era as a combination contact station and concession building, this structure combines the finest attributes of National Park Service design. Here, the CCC boys who built the structure pose in front of the nearly completed building. Henry Huntenburg (standing, in the

center, with a bow tie) was a camp mechanic. Today, the building serves as the nature and visitor center and retains most of its original design features, including the stonework and timber construction. (Courtesy Barbara Morse, Patricia Morse, and Joan Fairchild.)

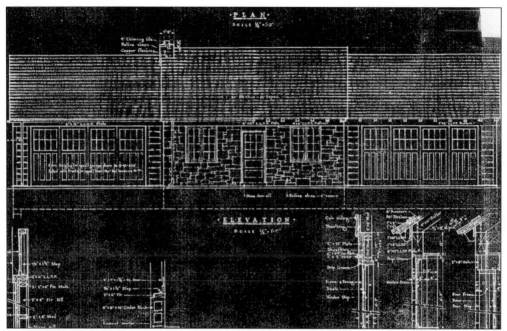

CCC boys built a new stone maintenance and equipment storage building that still survives and is used for the same purposes. It is believed that CCC boys removed some of the former iron miners' homes near Hacklebarney Pond in 1940 and used the materials for projects at Hacklebarney. (Courtesy Voorhees State Park.)

Because it is protected from the elements, the original CCC-carved "Work Shop" sign still hangs over the entrance to the shop. (Courtesy Voorhees State Park.)

This stone staircase is located a short distance from the nature center and proceeds from the main trail down to Trout Brook. Another set of stairs began near the concession building and joined the main trail into the park. After 1941, those stairs were moved to create a new staircase from the rest room facilities down to the main park trail. (Courtesy Voorhees State Park.)

Most of the trail network the park inherited from the original Borie donation was improved by the CCC boys. John Gray and Adolphe Borie had laid out and created the original trail plan. At least one new trail was proposed to get visitors to Lookout Hill, a promontory overlooking the Black River, but it was never built. (Reprinted from *We Can Take It: A Short Story of the CCC.*)

Four footbridges were constructed by the CCC boys, including this handsome timber bridge over Trout Book. (Courtesy Voorhees State Park.)

A new water supply was built in 1939, incorporating a 10,000-gallon concrete reservoir connected by almost 13,500 feet of pipe to 15 drinking fountains throughout the park. Unfortunately, the system is no longer functional, although many of the water fountains remain. (Courtesy Voorhees State Park.)

In addition to those built by the state, the CCC built more fireplaces along the trails at Hacklebarney, using standard National Park Service designs. Today, a number of those fire pits remain, and there are about 100 contemporary fire grills visitors can use. Camping was not allowed under the original deed restrictions, nor is it today. (Courtesy Voorhees State Park.)

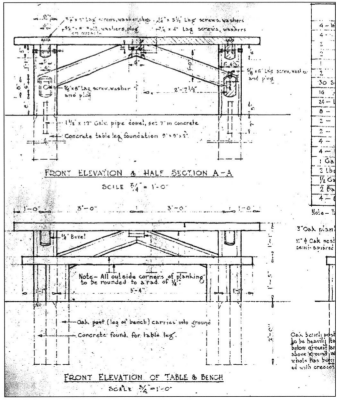

The National Park Service used a design for picnic tables that was more rustic than the state had used previously. The CCC boys built a number of picnic table-and-bench combinations at both parks. In the months following the closing of the CCC camp, the state finished a number of uncompleted projects, including building 75 picnic tables and several comfort stations and footbridges. (Courtesy Voorhees State Park.)

By 1940, fewer men were signing up for the CCC because of the better-paying jobs in the defense industry and because of the military buildup across America. In 1941, Pearl Harbor was attacked and America's resources were focused on winning the war. About 75 percent of the men who served in the CCC also served in World War II. (Courtesy Center for Research Libraries Collection.)

John Parichuk, a former Company 1268 enrollee, served in the U.S. Army in both the European and Pacific theaters. After the rationing, the war bond drives, and the worldwide destruction, the nation wanted to start anew, leaving the Depression and its memories behind. Most forgot about the CCC, although Pres. Franklin D. Roosevelt had always hoped that 5,000 CCC camps would be maintained permanently after the war. (Courtesy John Parichuk.)

96

## Seven

# HACKLEBARNEY TODAY

Hacklebarney State Park has always been a very different place than Voorhees. It continues to be a popular park for those who like more primitive and mysterious settings. It began its life as a pedestrian park and remains the same today. The National Park Service and CCC boys created a number of features promoting that legacy that are still used by the park's visitors as they take part in activities along the Black River, and the Trout and Rinehart Brooks. In more recent decades, new visitor amenities have been built, and visitation has continued to increase.

Since the original 32-acre donation in 1924, the park has grown to 977 acres. Beginning in 1964, the state began to acquire more land farther downstream. Additional properties have been obtained since then through donations and purchases by the Green Acres program, creating a corridor along the Black River. A 465-acre section of the park was placed in the Natural Area System in 1978.

One can imagine Adolphe Borie enjoying watching fly fishermen cast their lines on the Black River and knowing that the special haven he donated eight decades ago is still an exceptional place, used by thousands every year. He would also be pleased that the women he intended to honor with his original donation are still remembered. The other donors who followed Borie would also be pleased to know that the original intent of their respective endowments is still being carried out by the Division of Parks and Forestry.

Today, the CCC-built concession building, now known as the Nature Center, is still the first place that visitors stop, and various displays are available for viewing there. Mounted on the left side is a cast-iron sign, similar to the one at Voorhees State Park. (Courtesy Voorhees State Park.)

When the state's landscape architect closed out his CCC files on the projects at Voorhees and Hacklebarney, he called for more latrines, trail side shelters, trail and stream improvements, additional fireplaces and picnic sites, and the installation of directional signage. New rest rooms were built by the state in 1942 with materials left by the National Park Service. (Courtesy Voorhees State Park.)

In the late 1970s, the state undertook a major effort to upgrade the various parks and their sanitary facilities throughout the park system. This rest room, near the park's main entrance, was enlarged and improved during that time. (Courtesy Voorhees State Park.)

In the 1970s, two federally funded youth agencies were created to undertake projects in both federal and state parks across the country. They were the Youth Conservation Corps (YCC) and the Young Adult Conservation Corps (YACC). The YACC worked on projects at Hacklebarney and Voorhees, and one of the surviving construction projects is this storage shed. Both agencies were drastically curtailed in 1981, although the YCC still fulfills its mission. (Courtesy Voorhees State Park.)

In more recent years, projects have been completed that, with their reliance on the use of the rustic style that was so popular in the 1930s, are evocative of the CCC era. A new park bench, pictured here, is located along the Black River and is a great place to relax. (Courtesy Walter Rittger.)

Hacklebarney has over 100 picnic tables located throughout the park. Today, visitors can take advantage of a network of interlocking trails that total five miles in length and can be used by those with a range of abilities and interests. During the winter months, cross-country skiing is also permitted. Over 120,000 people visit Hacklebarney each year. (Courtesy Voorhees State Park.)

Both parks provide interpretive staff to educate the public about cultural and natural resources. There are over 100 bird species and a number of endangered species living in the park. Among the wildlife found in the parks are black bear, woodchucks, deer, and fox. (Courtesy Voorhees State Park.)

The Black River, which cascades through boulders in hemlock-lined ravines, cuts through Hacklebarney State Park. With its excellent trout fishing, it is a favorite for anglers. There are also two other wild trout streams in the park—the Trout Brook and Rinehart Brook. At Voorhees, Willoughby Brook is designated as a "Wild Trout Stream." (Courtesy Voorhees State Park.)

Hunters can also use both Hacklebarney and Voorhees in specific, designated hunting areas or "hunting zones." Small game, pheasant, turkey, grouse, and deer can be taken at the appropriate time of the year. A special use permit is granted to the Essex Fox Hounds, an equestrian organization. (Courtesy Bruce De Bacco.)

This type of vehicle, known as a "mule," is used in both parks to transport materials to and from the job site. The CCC-era equipment and maintenance building are in the background and are still used. (Courtesy Walter Rittger.)

# *Eight*
# VOORHEES TODAY

In 1944, a major goal of the original National Park Service plan was accomplished with the purchase of 105 acres of land owned by Dora Deutch. This parcel joined together the Hill Acres and Hoppock Tracts. After World War II, the state continued to develop the resources at Voorhees as additional tracts were acquired. This created a buffer around the park, which allowed it to expand and add to its facilities. The management organization of each of the parks has been altered over the years, but today, Hacklebarney and Voorhees are managed as a single unit.

Beginning in 1951 and continuing to the present day, a relationship between the park and disadvantaged or physically challenged young people has been maintained. For almost 30 years, the home of former Gov. Foster Voorhees served as a camp for the physically challenged. In more recent decades, it has been home to a Juvenile Justice Commission facility.

Voorhees would probably be delighted to know that his farm is now a multipurpose park that draws many people away from their more urban or suburban settings. Most of the park is now accessible to the public and appeals to many different interests. Visitors can hike, enjoy wonderful vistas, camp, have a picnic, visit an observatory, or just drive on nicely designed roads built by the CCC. One cannot help but think that Voorhees would have loved the idea of the CCC and the projects that they completed, particularly the planting of trees.

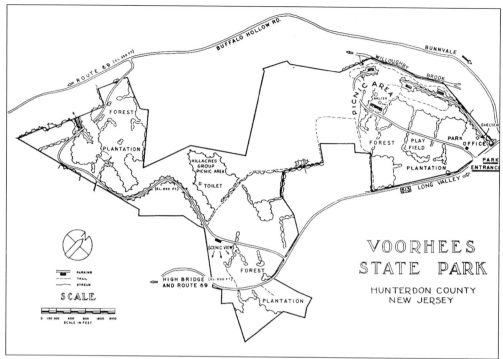

In the years since the intensive effort of the CCC, a number of new facilities have been created at Voorhees, including campgrounds, an observatory, a fitness course, group picnic areas, and two cross-park trails. This early 1960s map shows what Voorhees looked like in the years following the CCC era. (Courtesy Voorhees State Park)

Upon the death of the governor in 1927, his longtime housekeeper, Margaret Umfried, was given life rights to the house and surrounding grounds, as was the governor's brother Nathaniel, a physician. A widow who originally came from Germany, Umfried lived in the house until her death in 1951. She is buried in the Riverside Cemetery in Clinton. (Courtesy Voorhees State Park.)

With the death of Margaret Umfried, the Voorhees home was cleared of the governor's personal belongings, including the pen he used to call out the National Guard in 1898, and the Bible upon which he took the oath of office. In 1951, the Crippled Children Camp Association set up its operations in the former governor's mansion. (Courtesy Voorhees State Park.)

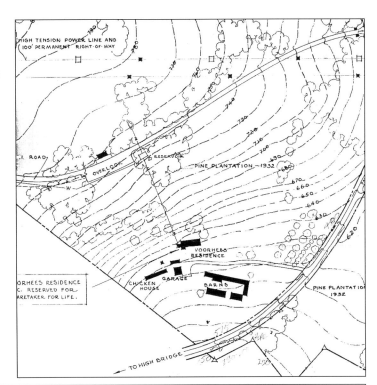

The five cabins seen here were erected in 1953, and other former farm buildings and the mansion were converted into dormitories and a shop. In 1955, the John V. Kenny Camp for Physically Handicapped Children of Jersey City, a non-profit organization, ran a summer program on the grounds around the former governor's mansion. A dining hall and new pool were built in 1958. (Courtesy Voorhees State Park.)

September 11, 1967

David B. Eckwielen
Supervisor, Region 7
Voorhees State Park
Lebanon, New Jersey

Dear Dave,

We wish to extend our sincerest thanks for
the use of the facilities during the summer
of 1967.  Without them our camping program would have bee incomplete.  You are
to be commended for the many fine
improvements and new services your park
has presented to the campers at A. Harry
Moore Camp and the public in general.

We hope to continue this fine relationship
in the coming years.

Sincerely,

Edward T. Spencer
Edward T. Spencer
Program Director

# A. HARRY MOORE CAMP
## JERSEY CITY STATE COLLEGE
### Route 513  High Bridge, N.J.  TEL. 638-8384

In 1963, Jersey City State College assumed responsibility for the camp. The camp was renamed to honor A. Harry Moore (1879–1952), a three-term governor of New Jersey. Since his term as park commissioner in Jersey City decades before, Moore had supported programs for physically challenged children. In 1931, the A. Harry Moore School for Crippled Children in Jersey City was dedicated to meet the educational needs of physically challenged children. Students from the school served as counselors for the camp, which remained open until 1977. (Courtesy Voorhees State Park.)

In 1965, a new resource was developed in the park by the New Jersey Astronomical Association. The organization was founded by seven men who had a passion for stargazing, astronomy, and building telescopes. The men leased 14 acres from the state and began working on a fund-raising program to construct an observatory. After four years, the observatory was completed and opened to the public. (Courtesy New Jersey Astronomical Association.)

This flag was flown to the Moon onboard Apollo 11
America's First Lunar Landing
JULY 20, 1969

Presented to New Jersey Astronomical Association
November 27, 1970

By *Buzz Aldrin*
Edwin E. Aldrin, Jr.
NASA Astronaut

The facility is officially named the Paul Robinson Observatory after one of the group's founders and early leaders. Several additions have been built, including the visitor and space exhibit room, which honors Col. Edwin "Buzz" Aldrin, the second American astronaut to set foot on the moon. Aldrin, a Montclair native, has visited the site. (Courtesy New Jersey Astronomical Association.)

Construction of the first stage of the complex was completed in 1985. The observatory at Voorhees houses the largest privately owned telescope in the state. Run entirely by volunteers, the New Jersey Astronomical Association continues to provide year-round educational programming for members and the general public alike. Distinguished lecturers often come to the site to make presentations. (Courtesy New Jersey Astronomical Association.)

At Voorhees, the YCC provided day jobs, while the YACC was a residential program. The YACC used the buildings of the former A. Harry Moore camp for its program, which employed young people who were between 16 and 23 years old. They upgraded the park's facilities, refurbished the Voorhees mansion, which had fallen into disrepair, and installed a new heating system and water lines. (Courtesy Voorhees State Park.)

While at Voorhees, the YACC worked on timber stand improvements, including harvesting dead and dying trees, thinning, removing brush, and planting trees. Other YACC projects included the construction of pit toilets and fire rings, the clearing of campsites, the renovation of the park shop residence, the installation of culvert pipes, and the creation of the concrete signposts that are still used as the base of state park and forest signs across the state. (Courtesy Voorhees State Park.)

One of the YACC's most important contributions to Voorhees was the construction of a new park office, which was built with materials left over from other projects built around the state. There are plans to construct a new park office in 2005. The new office will provide adequate space for the park staff, and the current building will be dismantled. (Courtesy Voorhees State Park.)

The park office in use during the years following World War II was torn down in 1984, after the new YACC-built office opened across the street in 1981. The building was located where the current parking lot is. The CCC-built entrance sign is to the right and uses a standard National Park Service design. (Courtesy David Eckwielen.)

After the departure of the YACC, an agreement with the U.S. Department of Corrections Juvenile Services (now Department of Law, Public Safety, Juvenile Justice Commission) allowed for the former A. Harry Moore camp to be used as an alternate facility for minor offenders with juvenile status. From this agreement in 1983 came crews who perform tasks in Voorhees and other recreational areas nearby. Today, the governor's former library is a resource center for the young men who reside there. (Courtesy Juvenile Justice Commission.)

The governor's orchard was maintained until the late 1960s, when the former picnic area was cleared of its trees and the Hill Acres Group Picnic and Playground Area was created. (Courtesy Voorhees State Park.)

The only CCC-era pavilion that survives at Voorhees, pictured here, is at Hoppock Picnic Grove, and it has been altered substantially. A new concrete floor was placed on top of the former stone floor, and the timber posts were replaced with stone. Portions of the gabled ends of the building may date from the CCC era. (Courtesy Voorhees State Park.)

What happened to the other pavilions is not known, but they were probably demolished after they fell into disrepair. Today, only the foundation of this pavilion remains, across from the current park office. (Courtesy Voorhees State Park.)

Many of the CCC-built features, like the timber bridges, lasted long after 1941. Here, the bridge crossing the stream leading into Hoppock Pond is used by two park visitors in 1965. (Courtesy Voorhees State Park.)

Spread across several locations in Voorhees are various kinds of playground equipment, including swings for children, that have been installed over the years. Pictured here is a family enjoying the park in 1971. (Courtesy Voorhees State Park.)

Both parks have continued to upgrade their playground equipment so that it conforms to the latest in recreation standards and provides families with young children a place to enjoy the park. (Courtesy Voorhees State Park.)

More than 30 years passed without action after the first suggestion of creating campgrounds was made. By the late 1960s, however, consideration was given to constructing public campgrounds at Voorhees. They were constructed on the perimeter of the CCC-era ball field, now located on State Park Road. In all, there were 30 campsites. A group campsite was also located across the road from the Hoppock Picnic Grove. (Courtesy Voorhees State Park.)

In the late 1980s, the park was actively considering the creation of new campground facilities. As part of the final plan, a new gateway was proposed. After opposition from the community, however, the park moved the gateway back from the road, utilizing the original dimensions. The flagpoles were moved, the wall was moved back about 20 feet, and the roadway was widened. (Courtesy Voorhees State Park.)

In 1992, a total of 50 new family campsites and trailer sites were opened at the former Orchard Group Picnic Area. The sites at the ball field were eliminated and turned into picnic sites. Other enhancements included new sanitary facilities and the Vista Trail, built by local Boy Scouts. Since then, three shelters have been added, eliminating three of the family campsites. The sites include fire rings and picnic tables, and the campground has rest room facilities. (Courtesy Voorhees State Park.)

In 1980–1981, a new fitness circuit, designed by both the Division of Parks and Forestry and Blue Cross Blue Shield of New Jersey, was installed in the park. It was completely refurbished in 2003, and includes an exercise program with 18 stations on a one-mile path. (Courtesy Voorhees State Park.)

In 1987, the park acquired 62 acres along its northern boundary. The property consisted of open fields and two man-made ponds, including the one pictured and another near Buffalo Hollow Road. This photograph, taken during the 1960s, also shows an old farmhouse, which was demolished in 1991. A group picnic area was built on this parcel. (Courtesy Voorhees State Park.)

Today, the group picnic areas throughout the park are heavily used by many park visitors and groups. There are over 125 picnic tables located throughout Voorhees State Park for visitors to use. (Courtesy Voorhees State Park.)

The park is often used by local joggers and walkers. Hikers can take advantage of eight different trails in Voorhees, several of which have been Boy Scout projects. Pictured here is the dedication of the Cross Park Trail in 1993. Today, over 100,000 people visit Voorhees each year. (Courtesy Voorhees State Park.)

The Voorhees family name is also still remembered at the high school across the street from the park's main entrance. It was named for Ralph and his wife, Elizabeth Voorhees. Ralph Voorhees was the paternal uncle of Gov. Foster Voorhees. The school was built in the early 1970s and opened in 1975. Students from the school use the park for athletic activities. (Courtesy Voorhees High School and Voorhees State Park.)

RALPH VOORHEES
1838-1907

ELIZABETH RODMAN VOORHEES
1841-1924

Ralph Voorhees and his wife, Elizabeth Voorhees, gave liberally to the Dutch Reformed and Presbyterian churches in Hunterdon County, in addition to many other worthy causes. Another legacy of the family's name is Voorhees Township in Camden County. When Gov. Foster Voorhees signed the legislation to divide Waterford Township into separate communities in 1899, the residents of the newly created township promptly named their community after him. Today, it is a township of more than 28,000 people, 20 miles from Philadelphia. The township also has a municipal park called the Voorhees Playground, sometimes confused with the state park, and a Voorhees Middle School. (Courtesy Voorhees State Park.)

# Nine

# LOOKING TO THE FUTURE

The state's parklands are increasingly becoming an oasis in the midst of tremendous development and are important to people as places to get away from the pressures of modern day life. There is also activity going on near both parks that enhances them, including the Patriot's Path trail, which runs along the Black River, not far from Hacklebarney. Close to Voorhees are Spruce Run and Round Valley Recreation Areas. Although not successful, there was an attempt to link Ken Lockwood Gorge to Voorhees in the late 1980s. Two satellite properties near Voorhees were acquired in 2004. These properties are not contiguous to the park but will be managed by the park, along with other partners.

As we celebrate Hacklebarney and Voorhees State Parks, we also recognize the challenges facing both parks. Budget shortfalls loom. Heavy development on both of the parks' borders threaten visitors' experiences. Overuse remains another challenge. Land acquisitions can be contentious. Curiously, when most people think of Hacklebarney today, it is not because of the park's natural beauty but rather because Tony Soprano, of the popular HBO television show *The Sopranos*, dumped a victim's body at a "Hacklebarney State Park." Unfortunately, it is all too clear that television holds a stronger grasp on us these days than does the preservation of our natural resources.

As we look back over the decades, we see that, for the most part, the parks bear a successful record. As we look to the future, we do so with hope that the vision of the original park donors will be maintained.

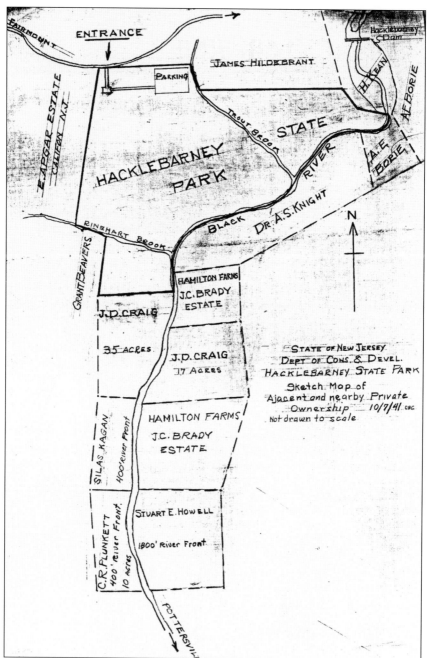

Beginning in the 1930s, state and National Park Service officials and Adolphe Borie began a conversation, discussing options for acquiring significant sections of property along the Black River in order to create a much larger park corridor. This map was drawn as a result of those discussions. Unfortunately, Borie never lived to see his vision completed, although he maintained an active interest in the park through the 1940s. In the late 1930s, he moved to Santa Barbara, California, where he died on April 25, 1954. His wife, Sarah, died on February 22, 1955, and they were both buried in the Santa Barbara Cemetery. (Courtesy Voorhees State Park.)

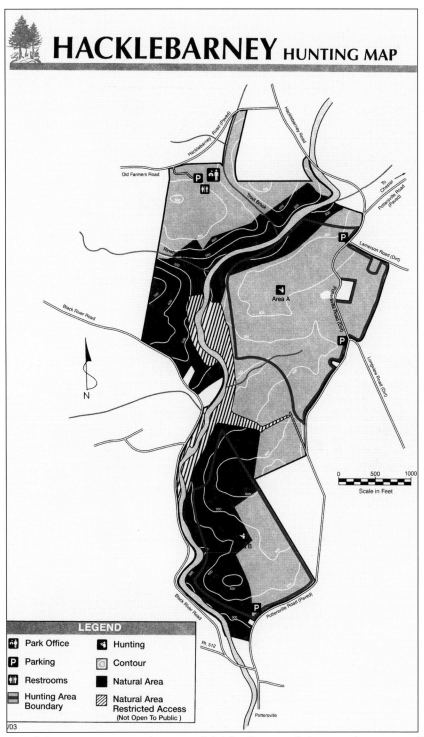

**HACKLEBARNEY** HUNTING MAP

**LEGEND**

| | | | |
|---|---|---|---|
| Park Office | | Hunting | |
| Parking | | Contour | |
| Restrooms | | Natural Area | |
| Hunting Area Boundary | | Natural Area Restricted Access (Not Open To Public) | |

The vision of those conversations between Adolphe Borie and the state has essentially been accomplished. It continues today, with land acquisitions being made by the Green Acres program and the New Jersey Conservation Foundation. (Courtesy Voorhees State Park.)

Probably Gov. Foster Voorhees's greatest contribution was not the donation of the state park, as important as that was, but the signature that allowed for the creation of the Palisades Interstate Park Commission, a unique bistate cooperative effort. It became the basis for the creation of Bear Mountain and Harriman State Parks, and for the preservation of the Palisades along the Hudson River. (Courtesy Cyndi and Dave Wood.)

In 1901, Voorhees also served on a commission that proposed the creation of State Forest Preserves. The creation of these preserves, or state forests, as they are now known, including Stokes State Forest in Branchville, was accomplished in 1905. In 1927, Voorhees promoted the process by donating his farm to be used for forestry demonstration projects. (Courtesy Voorhees State Park.)

The Voorhees family has a long tradition of public service and philanthropy dating back to the 1800s. The family continues its philanthropic efforts at such notable institutions as Rutgers, the state university, a legacy that dates back several generations. Pictured here is Ralph Voorhees, the grandson of Ralph and Elizabeth Voorhees, two very extraordinary people, at the home of Gov. Foster Voorhees, who himself represents the highest of the family's values. Not only did Foster Voorhees have a role on the Palisades Park Commission; several other family members did as well. John and Daniel Voorhees served on the commission in the years following its creation. Foster Voorhees also left a substantial estate, with bequests for family, friends, the Elizabeth General Hospital and Dispensary, Rutgers College, and the Woman's College of New Jersey (now Douglass College at Rutgers University). (Courtesy Voorhees State Park.)

A visitor cannot enter either of the parks today without passing a CCC-era project. More than 215,000 man-days and about $567,000 for supplies were spent during the eight years of work done by the boys at Hacklebarney and Voorhees—a bargain indeed. Many of the projects remain: the roads, trails, picnic areas, and buildings. Across the country, some $3 billion was spent on CCC projects. (Courtesy Center for Research Libraries Collection.)

One of the challenges facing both Voorhees and Hacklebarney is ongoing real estate development right up to the boundary lines of both parks, a trend occurring not only at these parks but also across the state and country. What was once a rural farming area in central New Jersey is quickly being built out, with large homes turning former farmland into suburban backyards. (Courtesy Voorhees State Park.)

Another challenge facing the parks is the necessity of conducting conservation procedures, like regularly prescribed burns. Neighbors concerned about the possibility that fires might jump the lines onto their properties or about the smell of smoke complain about such activities. Yet without these prescribed burns, forest undergrowth gets thick and creates greater fire hazards. (Courtesy Walter Rittger.)

One of the most critical issues facing all of the state's parks and forests is the level of funding needed to operate them. During these challenging fiscal times, the parks' patrons need to band together in order to create a greater awareness of the parks' maintenance and financial needs. (Courtesy Walter Rittger.)

There has been a renewed interest in the CCC during recent times. Although it is unlikely that this successful effort could be duplicated, one cannot help but hope that this fine conservation organization might be resurrected. Some groups, like the Student Conservation Association, the YCC, the YACC, and Americorps, trace their missions back to the CCC. (Courtesy Joseph Richardson.)

On October 26, 2003, a 70th-anniversary party was held at Voorhees State Park to commemorate the creation of the CCC. As part of the program, a guided tour of the former CCC camp was given. Here, Jack Woollis (left) and Joseph Catania, both former members of Company 1268, stand in front of the area their former barracks occupied. (Courtesy Voorhees State Park.)

Pictured are former CCC boys who attended the program, from left to right, Arthur Valente, Ken Fowler, Joseph Catania, Jack Woollis, Artie Riley, and Anthony Capizzi. Several of them were in Company 1268. Valente served at the CCC camp at High Point State Park. Michael Nalavany, also a former member of Company 1268, attended but is not pictured here. Bruno Goska, John Parichuck, and Ernest Nixon, all former enrollees of Company 1268 with a long interest in Voorhees State Park, could not attend. (Courtesy Voorhees State Park.)

Voorhees and Hacklebarney State Parks remain places that families can visit to catch a glimpse of nature, enjoy a waterfall, or escape from the pressures of modern day living. Both are places where people can commune with nature. Hopefully, that will continue to be the case for decades to come, because these are, after all, the people's parks. (Courtesy Voorhees State Park.)

# RESOURCES

## Books

Biddle, George. *Adolphe Borie*. Washington: The American Federation of Arts, 1937.

Binnewies, Robert. *Palisades: 100,000 Acres in 100 Years*. New York: Fordham University Press & Palisades Interstate Park Commision, 2001.

Case, Joan. *Images of America: Chester*. Portsmouth, New Hampshire: Arcadia Publishing, 1998.

Cohen, Stan. *The Tree Army: A Pictorial History of the Civilian Conservation Corps, 1933–1942*, rev. ed. Missoula, Montana: Pictorial Histories Publishing Company, 1996.

Good, Albert H. *Park and Recreation Structures*. New York: Princeton Architectural Press, 1999.

Honeyman, A. Van Doren, ed. *Northwestern New Jersey: A History of Somerset, Morris, Hunterdon, Warren and Sussex Counties*, vol. 4. New York: Lewis Historical Publishing Company, 1927.

Hoyt, Ray. *We Can Take It: A Short Story of the CCC*. New York: American Book Company, 1935.

*The Indians of the Hacklebarney Area*. Hacklebarney State Park file

Lowenthal, Larry. *Chester's Iron Heyday*. Chester, New Jersey: Chester Historical Society, 1980.

Merrill, Perry H. *Roosevelt's Forest Army: A History of the Conservation Corps 1933–1942*. Barre, Vermont: Northright Studio Press, 1981.

Osborne, Peter. *Images of America: High Point State Park and the Civilian Conservation Corps*. Portsmouth, New Hampshire: Arcadia Publishing, 2002.

Osborne, Peter. *We Can Take It! The Roosevelt Tree Army at New Jersey's High Point State Park 1933–1941*. Bloomington, Indiana: First Books Library, 2002.

Salmond, John A. *The Civilian Conservation Corps, 1933–1942: A New Deal Case Study*. Durham, North Carolina: Duke University Press, 1967.

Sary, Charles. *Hacklebarney State Park: History*.

Stellhorn, Paul, and Michael Birkner, eds. *The Governors of New Jersey 1664–1974*. Trenton, New Jersey: New Jersey Historical Commission, 1982.

*Stewardship through Historical and Natural Interpretation: Providing Memory and Meaning in New Jersey's Storied Places* (Draft). Trenton, New Jersey: Division of Parks and Forestry, New Jersey Department of Environmental Protection, 2002.

*Your CCC: A Handbook for Enrollees*. Washington, D.C.: Happy Days Publishing Company, 1940.

## Articles, Reports, and Unpublished Manuscripts

Mariette Siczewicz. *Memorandum—Civilian Conservation Corps*. State Parks Service, Voorhees State Park file, 1992.

Osborne, Peter, ed. *We Can Take It: The Roosevelt Tree Army at High Point State Park 1933–1941: Interviews With Former Civilian Conservation Corps Enrollees, Camp Kuser, Companies 216 & 1280*, vols. 1 and 2, rev. eds. 2000.

## Archives

Center for Research Libraries, 6050 South Kenwood Avenue, Chicago.

Department of Environmental Protection, 501 East State Street, Trenton, New Jersey.

Division of Parks of Parks & Forestry, State Park Service, New Jersey.

Franklin Delano Roosevelt Library, Hyde Park, New York.

Hacklebarney State Park, Long Valley, New Jersey.

Minisink Valley Historical Society, 138 Pike Street, Port Jervis, New York.

National Archives and Records Administration, 8601 Adelphi Road, College Park, Maryland.

National Personnel Records Center, 111 Winnebago Street, St. Louis.

New Jersey Historic Preservation Office.

Tidelands Management Bureau, Trenton, New Jersey.

Voorhees State Park, High Bridge, New Jersey.

## CCC Alumni Organizations

National Association Civilian Conservation Corps Alumni, 16 Hancock Avenue, St. Louis 63125.

## Miscellaneous

*Governor Foster Voorhees Historical Chronology*, Voorhees State Park file

## Internet

www.ancestry.com

www.encyclopedia-titanic.org

www.genealogy.com

www.njaa.org

www.vanvoorhees.org

## Addresses

Hacklebarney State Park, 119 Hacklebarney Road, Long Valley, New Jersey 07852-9525; (908) 879-5677.

Voorhees State Park, 251 County Road 513, Glen Gardner, New Jersey 08826; (908) 638-6969.